QUEENS OF THE RESISTANCE:
MAXINE WATERS

ALSO IN THE
QUEENS OF THE RESISTANCE SERIES

Elizabeth Warren
Alexandria Ocasio-Cortez
Nancy Pelosi

QUEENS OF THE RESISTANCE:

MAXINE WATERS

———————★———————

The Life, Times, and
Rise of "Auntie Maxine"

———————★———————

BRENDA JONES AND KRISHAN TROTMAN

PLUME

PLUME

An imprint of Penguin Random House LLC
penguinrandomhouse.com

Copyright © 2020 by Brenda Jones and Krishan Trotman

Penguin supports copyright. Copyright fuels creativity, encourages diverse
voices, promotes free speech, and creates a vibrant culture. Thank you for
buying an authorized edition of this book and for complying with
copyright laws by not reproducing, scanning, or distributing any part of it
in any form without permission. You are supporting writers and allowing
Penguin to continue to publish books for every reader.

Plume is a registered trademark and its colophon is a
trademark of Penguin Random House LLC.

Illustrations by Jonell Joshua
Interior Hand Lettering by Jonell Joshua and Dominique Jones

LIBRARY OF CONGRESS CATALOGING-IN-PUBLICATION DATA
has been applied for.

ISBN 9780593189870 (POB)
ISBN 9780593189917 (ebook)

Printed in the United States of America
1   3   5   7   9   10   8   6   4   2

BOOK DESIGN BY TIFFANY ESTREICHER

For Maxine Waters,
and all the Queens of the Resistance reading this

CONTENTS

You wanna be this Queen B
But ya can't be
That's why you're mad at me.
—Lil' Kim, "Big Momma Thang"

INTRODUCTION:
THE QUEENS OF THE
RESISTANCE SERIES

Dear Sis,

The Queens of the Resistance is a series that celebrates the life and times as well as the lessons and rise of our favorite sheroes and Queen Bees of politics. It's a celebration of the *boss*, the loud in their demands, and a rebellion against the long and tired patriarchy. They are the shining light and new face of the US government. The idea for the series began to germinate in 2016. Hillary Clinton was in the presidential race. She was top dog, Grade A. She was supposed to go all the way as the first female president. She had done everything right. In the 1960s, she switched parties when the civil rights movement was demonstrating that changing allegiance wasn't about betting on the winner but believing in a different vision for America's future. She married one of the most capable politicians of the twentieth century at the time, Bill Clinton, who would eventually appoint the first Black secretaries of commerce and labor and put women and minorities in many positions of power. She was considered most likely to be president when she gave a commencement speech during her graduation from Wellesley, then went on to graduate Yale Law at the head of her class. She was the first female partner of two law firms in Arkansas, First Lady of Arkansas, First Lady of the United States—but she didn't stop there. She became the first female US senator from New York, a seat that had primed Robert Kennedy to run for president, and one of the first female secretaries of states. She was the first woman *ever* to be nominated by a major political party to run for president. Even the political machine was oiled and greased to work in her favor. She had been generally considered one of the most qualified people ever to run for president, even by her opponents, but with all that going for her, somehow, some way, she didn't make it. *Sigh* You can't get more presidential than Hillary Clinton in 2016. She had it all, even the majority of popular votes in the 2016 election.

So what happened? Ha! Every woman knows what happened! Everybody laughed at her in 1995, when she appeared on the *Today* show and attributed the chop-down of her husband to a "vast right-wing conspiracy," but she was right. Who knew that while we were enjoying the moment, the wind beneath our wings after two terms—the first Black president, a time that had left us proximal to a variety of enjoyable mini multi-cultures—sushi, guacamole, break dancing—there was a group of malcontents intent on making America great again . . . "great" like the 1940s. And that meant forcing women back into the kitchen, padlocking the door, and throwing away the key. There'd be no need to vilify female candidates with memes, negative ads, and sucker punches like the opposition had to do to Hillary Clinton; the social stigma would do all the policing and policy work needed to keep women out of the ring and out of the way, so the boyz could rule, unchecked, unaccountable, and unrestrained. "Less for you, more for me" has always been a natural law in a capitalist society. It means getting rid of competition by every means necessary—deportation, mass incarceration, legislation, deprivation, deconstruction, and divestment, to name a few. Our sister Hillary was a woman who fell in the crosshairs of a right-wing machine dead set against any diversion from its outrageous plan—to stop collective action and make sure politics bends only to its will, not the people's. It didn't matter that Hillary was the smartest, the most prepared, or the first in this or that. Merit's not the point; it's compliance that matters, and Hillary was just too damn smart, too capable, too talented, for her own good. She had a vast right-wing conspiracy working against her, and they won . . . temporarily.

And that's where this series begins. Queens of the Resistance is as much an ode to the women as it is a celebration of a transcending political identity in America unlike history has ever shown us before.

With Love,
Brenda & Krishan

QUEENS OF THE RESISTANCE:
MAXINE WATERS

★ ★ ★ ★ ★ ★ ★ ★ ★ ★ ★

BORN

My mama taught me to fight if I had to, so I do.

—LECIA MICHELLE

RECLAIMING MY TIME

I got nothing to lose
It's just me against the world.
—Tupac, "Me Against the World"

As a Black woman, a feminist, and a fearless politician who never minces words when it comes to injustice, Auntie Maxine, dubbed by Millennials the Clap-Back Queen and Queen of Shade, is a ferocious, fiery leader who is unafraid to simultaneously rep "the hood" or wield the gavel like an anvil, and does not mind making men who run roughshod over the United States democracy squirm. She's seen it all, and has been through it all.

Maxine Waters, the longest serving Black woman in the US House of Representatives, has been in public service for more than forty years. She is the first woman and first African American chair of the House Financial Services Committee. Waters was first nicknamed Auntie Maxine at large back in 2017, after she told the nation that FBI Director James Comey had "no credibility." Her takedown of Comey went viral and she has been the voice many Americans post fist-pump emojis or nodding along from their sofas to "Preach!" Auntie Maxine always delivers *truth*, sis. This queen is not a friend of bowing or biting her tongue in the name of hierarchy. She will come for a president, an attorney general, whoever, anytime she smells injustice.

A very unwise man, Treasury Secretary Steve Mnuchin had to be schooled on how to conduct himself with a queen during a hearing in July 2017 when Auntie Maxine asked about his boss's shady ties to Russian banks. He tried to evade her question about why neither she nor her Democratic committee members had received a response about a letter they sent him months earlier, on May 23. Honey, excuse him because he was new and arrogant. He had just started his job in July—obviously he had not done his homework. He tried to offer Auntie some compliments and sweet talk to wobble around the question: "Ranking member Waters, first let me thank you for your service to California. Being a resident of California, I appreciate everything that you've done for the community there—"

"Thank you for your compliments about how great I am, but I don't want to waste my time on me," she said. It was simple: get to the point.

"I also want to thank you for the opportunity to meet with me today—"

"Reclaiming my time," she said, shutting down the nonsense.

He continued.

"Reclaiming my time," she repeated again, with a glare, stern and brittle.

He continued—

"Reclaiming my time."

Her eyes set like a hawk, almost piercing through him. "Reclaiming my time."

"Reclaiming my time."

She fired out the words, invoking a House procedure used in committee or on the House floor for retrieving allotted time when a witness or another politician is being elusive. Her words went viral as a reflection of a sentiment that a majority of the nation's voters felt about what appeared to be a morbid opening dance with President Donald Trump, and one that would only continue to get worse for years into his presidency. The American people were fed up with the BS, and Auntie Maxine said what 2.9 million voters (48.2 percent) all wanted to say to Trump: *Puhleeasse* Do. Not. Waste. Our. Time.

In the hearing, the chairman, at that time Jeb Hensarling, allotted Maxine Waters her time back. She thanked Mnuchin again for his "compliments" and proceeded with the same question. Why the heck hadn't he responded to the letter?

"I was going to answer that—" he offered. Was Maxine Waters going to participate in this child's play? No.

"Please just go straight to answering the question."

"Mr. Chairman," he said to Hensarling, as if giving her the hand and bypassing her, sis. "I thought when you read the rules that you acknowledged that I shouldn't be interrupted and that I would have—"

"Reclaiming my time," Auntie Maxine spat, then looking squarely in the face of the gulping man before her, she said, "What he failed to tell you was [that] when you're on my time, I can reclaim it."

And that, dear sister, is Auntie Maxine.

A GIRL FROM ST. LOUIS

*Long live the rose that grew from concrete
when no one else even cared.*
—Tupac, "The Rose That Grew from Concrete"

Auntie Maxine, given name Maxine Moore Carr, was born and came rumbling into the resistance on August 15, 1938, the fifth of her mother's thirteen children, in St. Louis, Missouri. Sis, of course it would be years before she grew into a queen, but this supernova rapped a story glittering with trails of courage from the moment she was born. She grew up facing a salty, racist world, but her family and community knew her worth, and they nurtured her.

Auntie Maxine's mother, Velma Lee Carr, was born in 1916 in Cotton Plant, Arkansas. Velma came of age when the soil was rich and cotton was king. A railroad line eventually changed the business of Cotton Plant from picking to processing, which gave a glimmer of hope to white businessmen, but of course life was still clouded for the workers, those who'd inherited brown skin.

The United States had already been ravaged by the poverty of the Great Depression for nearly ten years, and Jim Crow had ruled the South for almost seventy years.

Black people were looking for a champion, someone who would be bold enough to challenge the forces that confronted them, and the war being waged against them, in every quarter of American society. It seems perfectly fitting that the same year Auntie Maxine was born, a heavyweight champion and son of a sharecropper, Joe Louis, knocked out a German fighter, Max Schmeling, in the first round. Black Americans saw a champion in Joe Louis, but they had no idea that another champ had been born in St. Louis, one who would take their fight to Washington and win some of the most improbable victories.

Before Velma and her husband, Remus Carr, had Maxine, they'd lived in Pine Bluff, Arkansas, where a Black community had existed ever since the Civil War. Union Army forces had set up camp in Pine Bluff, which was at the time still Confederate territory, and it became a magnet for enslaved people who ran away, as well as freed African Americans seeking some level of safety. The army had to set up what were called "contraband camps" to create an organized space for all of them.

After the war ended, Pine Bluff became a place where a society of educated, skilled African Americans thrived. Missionary societies founded schools to educate freed people, and both adults and children began to gain an education. The Branch Normal School of Arkansas Industrial University was developed. A historically Black college, it ultimately became the University of Arkansas at Pine Bluff, the oldest and largest Historically Black Colleges and Universities (HBCU) in the state. Pine Bluff began to develop a bustling Black community with a thriving main street filled with Black-owned businesses—barbershops, banks, and bars. Wakanda is fictional, but places like Pine Bluff, Arkansas, or Tulsa, Oklahoma, were not, and they became staples for Black prosperity right in this country.

The spirit of Pine Bluff would live in the soul of Velma, and she'd spill it over into the hearts of her children. That spirit created the root of social justice that continues to fuel Maxine Waters today, the origin of her strength and hope for Blacks in America that stems from lands that her mother knew, like Pine Bluff.

When Velma was about ten years old, the Great Flood occurred. This seminal event would affect the lives of everyone in Pine Bluff. This Mississippi River flood was actually the first time in recent history when the levees broke, long before Hurricane Katrina. It devastated and swallowed the nearby crops and farmland, and the region struggled to recover, not knowing that just three years later, the 1929 stock market would crash hundreds of miles away in New York City, and the Great Depression would hang over the nation for more than a decade.

The region was battered, but it soldiered on, and through it all, St. Louis remained a bustling industrial city. Roosevelt's Works Progress Administration built a highway system that made travel between cities more accessible. St. Louis is right on the eastern edge of Missouri, one state away from Kansas, which had rejected slavery and represented a new frontier of freedom during the Civil War. With one hand in the South and the other in the North, Missouri played a middle position between the Union and Confederacy; it held two governments with representatives on both sides of the conflict, some serving in the US Congress and some serving in the Confederate Congress. By 1861, the Union gained control and Missouri was considered a Union state.

St. Louis was a sophisticated Black community, baby, which was assisted by a series of nine very industrious Free Masonic Lodges that invested in the community. They helped newly arriving Black migrants from farther south find jobs and housing, and offered relief for food and clothing. They also contributed to Black charities and supported the education of young people. By the 1930s, St. Louis Blacks had moved beyond the struggle to survive. They were soaring. Soon most prominent members of the community were part of one Masonic Lodge or another and African Americans flocked to the city to find culture, opportunity, and the support of a welcoming arena.

Education had been a staple of the Black community there

since before the Civil War. John Berry Meachum, a pastor of the First Baptist Church in St. Louis in 1827, created Lincoln Institute, the first school for African Americans in the city. Five more schools connected to African Methodist Episcopal and Black Baptist churches were created in St. Louis, and both denominations were active participants in the abolition of slavery from the 1840s. But unfortunately, sis, fear that educated Blacks would influence those who were still enslaved led to the passage of a law in Missouri making it illegal to educate African Americans inside the borders of the state.

Pastor John Meachum remained undaunted and set up a school on a barge on the Mississippi River bordering St. Louis—outside the jurisdiction of the state. It was an act of resistance, a squeeze to the muscle needed to upend the circumstances caused and residue created by slavery. After the war, Missouri made it mandatory that all boards of education support African American education, and twelve schools for African Americans, including Summer High School, were born. St. Louis was a city invested in Black opportunity.

Soon enough, Remus and Velma, Maxine Waters's parents, made their way to St. Louis with the children. Life would continue to unfold quickly for Velma; Maxine's father left the family when Maxine was two. But Velma was familiar with survival. As a child she had lost her mother when she was only five years old, and was raised by her grandparents,

Doke and Florence Eldridge. Now Velma went on with determination and courage to raise her children the best way she could. Soon she married again, to Samuel Willie Moore.

Prior to the move to St. Louis, the family spent a short time in Kinloch, Missouri, the first African American community to be incorporated in the state. In an interview with *Lenny Letter*, Auntie Maxine remembers Kinloch with great pride: "It was a very warm community where everybody knew everybody. We were accustomed to Black entrepreneurs where we shopped at our grocery store and at our bakery. Our schoolteachers were black. We had a very positive image of Black leadership throughout our community."

When she says "our," what Auntie Maxine means is Black-owned, *otay*.

Today, Auntie Maxine is known as a shrewd protector, *fly* as hell in a suit and unassuming with that bright smile. But don't be fooled. Like a honey badger, she will take out any rival that steps in her den, and digest his bones and feathers if he starts acting up. It was in the community of Kinloch that she started developing those skills, where she was first inspired to be the tough leader who could still love, and be tender, and champion her people to persevere yet equally rebel against the wrongdoings. Kinloch was enveloped by Blackness due to segregation, and racism was a tool to withhold the Black community from rising up, but like baby whales the children of the community swam on the backs of the Black elders and moved along in life, anyway. Auntie Maxine loves Black men and can quote their wisdom, from Frederick Douglass to Tupac Shakur, but it was specifically the Black women she credits for making the difference in her life. This positive image of what it meant to be African American and a woman forged in Waters, in her formative years, the idea of being a fierce activist and capable leader for African American people and communities around the world.

VELMA EVENTUALLY SETTLED her children permanently in St. Louis, and by the time Maxine was two years old, Velma was a single mother of thirteen living in one of the first housing projects in the country. They were on and off welfare, as Maxine puts it, depending on if Velma could uphold a job with all the demands of motherhood and childcare on her back. The housing projects themselves had a complicated history. Though poverty existed in St. Louis, so did self-respect, and examples of success abounded among people who found themselves part of the working class. Determined, however, to break up the basis of their power, white separatists began to develop plans to raze entire Black neighborhoods under the guise of urban renewal. So-called urban renewal would destroy the intricate networks of community that had been a decades-old framework of support that ensured the poor were never destitute, hungry, or without.

The largest so-called developments were built shortly after World War II, just as St. Louis had become a mecca for Black culture due to a community of extremely successful African American individuals living there. Miles Davis, who was born around the same time as Maxine, must have spent a lot of time in St. Louis, which was just across the river from his birthplace. A young Charlie Parker, creator of bebop, visited from Kansas City. It was a cultural center, and as a little girl, Maxine Waters was in the midst of it.

But there were also many challenges. During the 1940s and '50s, the city of St. Louis had more than 85,000 families living in housing tenements, many with only communal toilets. The projects were racially segregated, and as middle-class whites were leaving the city, low-income Black families were moving in (and it remained segregated until 1956 when Auntie Maxine graduated high school, but more on that later).

At a young age, Auntie Maxine became accustomed to visits from social workers, who'd often come by to examine and inspect the welfare recipient's home. "I was never ashamed of it," said Waters, who speaks openly and respectfully of her childhood, "but I knew that it was not enough. Being almost a ward of the state in the sense of looking to someone for money to live on was not a quality way to live. I wanted more than that."

Young Maxine saw herself in the eyes of the Black women who were the teachers and community organizers. They were the ones who helped her mother. Ultimately, even as a child, Little Maxine knew that she would one day be a badass professional. She wanted to be either a dancer, like Katherine Dunham, or a social worker. In an interview with Shonda Rhimes, she said, "Yeah, lots of dancing. We had a community center. All of the neighborhoods had their own community center in St. Louis, which was really a wonderful thing for low-income neighborhoods to have a central place for activities and sports activities. They had dance there and we had a dance teacher. We did ballet, interpretive dance, and all of that. So yeah, I wanted to be a dancer. I loved Katherine Dunham. I also wanted to be a social worker because, when we were on welfare, we were visited by social workers. It seemed like they had so much power."

Katherine Dunham was one of the most successful African American dancers in history. She was an anthropologist who traveled to Haiti, Martinique, Jamaica, and Trinidad and Tobago while on a Julius Rosenwald and Guggenheim Fellowship to study the ethnography of African American dance. On her travels she developed new flavorful Afrocentric techniques that she'd share by founding one of the first Black ballet companies in the country, called Ballets Nègres. She toured all over the world and appeared in iconic Black plays and films such as *The Emperor Jones*. To a girl like Maxine in St. Louis, Katherine Dunham was fantastical.

But it was the career professional in Little Maxine's real life who made an even deeper impression. And she proclaimed at a very early age that *that* was who she wanted to be.

"The social worker was the authority figure I saw in my life during those days on welfare . . ." said Waters in her interview with Rhimes. "And I thought that if I could only be a social worker, then I could really help people."

To her, social workers were like mini marching Thors; they provided resources that supported families like hers, and they had all the control and authority to decide who received how much and which month. Even though they were nosy as hell, and Maxine would wince in her loafers if they happened to ask her one of their probing questions when they came snooping around the house, she respected their work. She envied their power to be able to bring change into existence. She also understood the power of paying it forward, a value that her mother taught her and that the culture of Black St. Louis demonstrated. She couldn't know it yet, but her memories of those social workers would inspire her all the way to Congress.

Her mother utilized the only support she could—public assistance from the government. And raising a family in poverty did not kill her spirit; Velma was an indomitable Black woman and Maxine's anchor. She said to *Essence*, "My mother was my original example of a strong Black woman . . . Although she was not educated, having only gone to third grade, she knew how to set an example and a foundation."

Despite her circumstances, Velma knew how to love on her children and community, and she had a heart big enough to care for so many. Her mother bestowed on Maxine the greatest gifts a young brown-skinned girl could have: self-respect and social responsibility. "Try to have a decent quality of life not only for yourself but for those around you," Velma would tell the future congresswoman. Despite tough circumstances, Velma had the love of her children and community, and she had a big heart, one that understood how to care for so many, just like Auntie Maxine. Velma bestowed on Maxine the greatest gift a young brown-skinned girl could have: self-love. She taught all her children to speak up for themselves and fight back against unfairness, because she knew their lives would be full of challenges.

No matter what, like the people of Pine Bluff and Kinloch, they should pound the pavement, blow through the roof, cut through the dirt if they had to.

Fighting back would be necessary.

LIFT EV'RY VOICE AND SING

Thou who has by Thy might
Led us into the light
—James Weldon Johnson, "Lift Ev'ry Voice and Sing"

Under Velma's steadfast guidance and support, Maxine entered school, attending James Weldon Johnson Elementary. In 1920, James Weldon Johnson had become the first executive secretary of the NAACP, serving until 1930, and died in a traffic collision in 1938, the year Maxine was born. He was a poet and writer who authored the lyrics to the Negro National Anthem, "Lift Ev'ry Voice and Sing." The anthem was a key foundation of young Maxine's upbringing, and its inspiration would feed her potential. In the book *Lift Every Voice and Sing* by Julian Bond and Sondra Kathryn Wilson, she shares,

> *My name is Maxine Waters, but when I sing the Negro National Anthem, I revert to Maxine Carr . . . I revert to*

the little girl in St. Louis, Missouri, who attended the James Weldon Johnson Elementary School from the fourth to the eighth grade. I feel a special kinship with James Weldon Johnson and the Negro National Anthem. I sang the anthem on days when I trotted to school in the rain and snow without rainwear, boots, or gloves. I sang the Negro National Anthem when I was hungry—I sang the Negro National Anthem when my tooth was hurting because of an exposed cavity—I sang the Negro National Anthem when I did not know there was a future for a little Black girl with twelve sisters and brothers. I felt strong when I sang the Negro National Anthem, although I didn't understand the meaning of the words.

The James Weldon Johnson Elementary School was a three-story brick building that sat at the corner of Laclede and Ewing Streets in St. Louis. Maxine's sixth-grade teacher, Ms. Stokes, a middle-aged woman with gray hair, would play the piano as her class sang along. Next to the social worker who had first stoked her ambition, Ms. Carter, her fifth-grade math teacher, and Ms. Stokes were important Black women who had a major impact on Maxine, and who molded in her the confidence to get where she is today.

Most of the teachers lived in the community, so they knew the families of their students well. If the students went along with their parents to church, their teachers would be there too. If they were out shopping with their families, Ms. Stokes, Ms. Carter, or any other teacher could appear. It was the 1950s; differences between teacher and student circumstances were not so apparent, because nearly every Black resident was in the same boat, segregated and discriminated against. As a community, there was a continuous resistance and sense of striving in the air, both socially and economically, and the close relationships between the teachers and students meant teachers were very aware of the children's circumstances. The shared intimacy of community left much less room for that awful disconnect between teachers and students—stereotypes, objectification, or fear of the students that can happen in classrooms today.

Some today fear Auntie Maxine, who is clear about the respect that she demands. She won't take anything less than 100 percent of what she deserves—whether one is directly addressing her or the people of the United States with their mess, Bill O'Reilly. If she's not feelin' it, we will hear about it. And she has no qualms about being a Black woman who is angry. "I have a right to my anger, and I don't want anybody telling me I shouldn't be [angry], that it's not nice to be, and that something's wrong with me because I get angry."

It goes back to her teachers and the Black women in her community that Waters learned to be bold in her demands. These women demanded that the children excel and be disciplined. And today, much of what we see Maxine Waters

exercise is not anger—it's just showing those unapologetic expectations. Her teachers were preparing Black children for a world that was hostile to them, doing more than educating them academically but preparing them socially and culturally for a world that would not welcome them, where they would have to struggle to assert their dignity and worth.

Maxine described it this way in the book *The Right Words at the Right Time*: "They spanked us when we were bad; but when we were good, they rewarded us with special lessons that went beyond the typical three-Rs curriculum. They taught us old Negro spirituals; they recited great oratory and took us on journeys through the world's rich cultural arts."

Due to discrimination that closed other careers to them, some of the most educated, well-prepared African American women taught in the elementary and high schools. In the 1940s and '50s, it was very difficult for even a college-educated African American to get a professional job. And Black women were doubly restricted due to gender and race. Many of the college-educated Black women teaching in high school classrooms were actually providing college-level training and preparation, imparted with a sophisticated understanding of a subject matter and the culture at large that prepared their students extremely well. Hence, Maxine Waters. Also their teachers had faced the same hardships and could teach them the values needed to achieve success. So much of what was required related to identity, the capacity to process ugly messages that would try to define them in the world and reject those messages as inconsistent with their own understandings of who they were. This sense of identity and worth was an invaluable foundation for Waters, who would go on to defend the least and the left-out so well against those who saw their existence as a threat.

Waters remembers her teachers as not only smart and resourceful but also loving and kind.

The academic and cultural training of the St. Louis Black public schools from that era permeated the community of Black St. Louis residents. There was a sense of legacy in this well-established society that mandated preparing future generations for the continuing struggle African Americans across the nation had waged over decades—a struggle that demanded American society live up to its ideals of equal justice. This pride of heritage gave them a platform of confidence to outdistance their humble beginnings, even poverty itself, and rise to meet the great opportunities waiting for them in their lives. Their teachers taught limitless possibility and exemplified the truth of their existence; that they were equal to anybody and just as capable, and at times even more prepared to meet the challenges that would define their future. Yes, honey, yaass!

Maxine's math teacher, Louise Carter, was "beyond her skill at teaching math," Maxine told *Jet*. "Ms. Carter was a very loving woman who saw her responsibility as above and beyond teaching in the classroom."

One day, Maxine discovered she was close to missing a school picnic because her mother wouldn't be able to get her ready in time. She had twelve other kids to tend to, after all. Hearing of her predicament, "Ms. Carter came and she would not leave without me," Waters said. She took Maxine to her own home, washed and braided her hair, got her clothes together, and took her to the picnic so that she could participate in the fun with other kids. That kind of fierce love, sis, the kind that would extend itself and be sensitive and delicate enough to understand the deep disappointment of a little girl who would miss the picnic, was what Maxine Waters grew up knowing, and would then employ in herself as a woman. Her teacher understood Maxine's circumstances, but she would not allow them to define her existence. In so many ways, that is what equality meant: the ability to join in with others and share the struggles as well as the delights of life. The impact of Carter's love has stuck with Maxine throughout her career. "Ms. Carter had high expectations for me; and—especially after that picnic—I tried my best to live up to them."

This confidence, belief in the unknown, and vision for the future is why Congresswoman Waters is beloved in the notorious parts of Los Angeles, even within those most feared neighborhoods of forgotten stucco and concrete buildings compiled row by row with brown families chafed by poverty and violence. She is respected there because she knows and understands her constituents are not defined by their circumstances—be they gangbanger or accountant—but knows they have the power, just as she did, to define themselves, no matter what society said about them.

IT WAS AN assignment in Ms. Stokes's sixth-grade class that would instill in young Maxine a tremendous lesson of success—and how to *in the voice of Drake* go from the bottom to the top. Ms. Stokes was someone the kids secretly called an old maid. But in hindsight, Maxine says, "She was full of warnings and advice. She was stern and loving. She was as critical as she was complimentary. And she had a keen, almost clairvoyant, sense of her students. Most important, though, Ms. Stokes helped us to develop confidence in ourselves."

In the book *The Right Words at the Right Time*, Waters describes a day when Ms. Stokes assigned the class a health and nutrition report. She communicated her high expectations and what the final product should look like: "thorough, informative, and 'presentable to any person in the City of St. Louis.'" Whoa, it was a high-sounding declaration of standards for students in the sixth grade, but that's not what worried Maxine. She was worried about money. "Ordinarily most of my classmates submitted their reports in fancy, store-bought notebooks or binders. But because I was poor, I never had the means to purchase such supplies. Naturally, I fretted that my report would not have the visual flair of my classmates' submissions."

She decided to design her own folder from magazine clippings and use recycled construction paper that had been previously given to her by Ms. Stokes. To bind the pages together, she used a hole puncher and colored yarn that had been given to her by a classmate. With no financial means at all, little Maxine had created something beautiful.

When she handed in the report to Ms. Stokes, her teacher smiled big and wide, and held the folder up to the class. "Look at this, class. Where there is a will there is a way," Ms. Stokes cried, and those words have never left Maxine Waters, and have become her mantra ever since.

IT WAS NESTLED under the gaze of strong Black queens that a young girl was shown that anything was possible. At an early age, Maxine decided to work part time to help her mother, whom everyone affectionately referred to as "Ma Dear."

She started with babysitting and, by 1951, when she was thirteen years old, she was busing tables at Thompson's restaurant, a white-owned establishment. The restaurant was located outside of the nest of her community, where she saw the true face of racism. In the world at large, in white St. Louis, a city deeply anxious about the success and capability of Blacks residing within its limits, the impact of racism was that much more bitter . . . and disgusting. There were the signs, WHITE WAITING and COLORED WAITING. Men and women—not just a little girl like her, but actual grown-ups, people she looked up to—were verbally abused and degraded by practices that sought to tear down the type of pride that her teachers had so lovingly built up. Maxine ate her meals in the basement like the other Black restaurant and factory workers. These experiences left indelible images in her mind, and she understood exactly what her teachers had been preparing her for.

Young Maxine concentrated on school and work, but a couple years prior to her job at Thompson's, Black women and men, along with white allies, at Congress of Racial Equality (CORE) had organized lunch-counter demonstrations in St. Louis department stores, and by the mid-1940s, they'd attained the right to dine in basement cafeterias. They also staged marches to get better jobs, for example, as telephone operators, where the laws prevented the Black women from working alongside white women. They were hired but placed in separate offices and sometimes even separate buildings. But segregation remained even after 1954. Young Maxine was able to work at Thompson's on the coattails of civil rights activists, but there was still plenty left to endure.

In 1956, she graduated from Vashon High School, the second high school in the city of St. Louis that served Blacks. The school was named after George Boyer Vashon, the first African American to graduate from the famously abolitionist school Oberlin College. In Waters's yearbook, she was named the student most likely to be Speaker of the House of Representatives. *Mhmm.* You have to look back in time and wonder where that incredibly admirable—and nearly prophetic—superlative came from. Though Maxine would live in a time that would usher in the first female Speaker to accept the gavel and the first Black president, never in the history of the country had there ever been examples like that to look to. It must have been the high expectations of her community, mother, and teachers in which she walked that allowed her classmates to look beyond the reality of the moment, to see that she'd aspire to achieve heights that would break barriers and open doors. Although it certainly wasn't just outside influence—it was the iron will of young Maxine herself, the one who went the extra mile to cover her report so beautifully, and the one who kept working all summer in a restaurant full of racist customers to help support her family.

So when someone like Trump or whomever gets tripped up over the congresswoman's no-nonsense attitude, they should remember where she comes from, and why she is so dang woke. Auntie Maxine calls it like she sees it, and it's because she's seen a lot. She's the inspiration for hashtags like #BlackWomen AtWork(!), established in 2017 when there was a day of vicious alt-right attacks on two highly successful Black women, Auntie Maxine and White House correspondent April Ryan, in which conservative talk show host Bill O'Reilly poked fun at Waters's hair (obviously envious because of his balding egg) and a salty Sean Spicer, the former White House press secretary, asked Ryan to "stop shaking her head again" after she disputed his account of White House activities. Activist Brittany Packnett tweeted for Black women to start sharing their #BlackWomenAtWork moments—*hell yeah, thank you for asking*—in which we surely did have a lot to tell, and the post went viral and inspired a national conversation about white privilege.

Black women like television anchor Tamron Hall and former chair of the Democratic National Committee Donna Brazile participated, and Auntie Maxine tweeted back to the tribe her famous words that served as a united sentiment among Black women: "I am a strong Black woman. I cannot be intimidated, and I'm not going anywhere."

Auntie Maxine's experiences have blessed her with the chutzpah to call out O'Reilly and the Trump administration minions, as she "encourage[s] others to see [Trump] for what he is: basically a bully, an egotistical maniac, a liar and someone who did not need to be president."

As Auntie Maxine said at an event in the bookstore Busboys and Poets in DC, if Trump could ever escape his patriarchal cocoon to understand the strength of the heritage that she has drawn on to carry her legacy, then he'd know for sure that there's no reason for someone like *her* to back down to someone like *him*.

But Trump doesn't need to get it, ever, because the resistance has arrived to clean out the pods of men like him. With Queens of the Resistance, like Auntie Maxine, at the center of the movement, one who lived to witness both the end of legalized segregation and the entrance of America's first Black president, who has led the way for the Squad and the number of women and people of color in Congress, we will only continue to prove successful in making toast of Trumpist cheese heads. In 2018, 575 women decided to run for the House and Senate, 60 percent more than those who ran in 2016, and there hadn't been that many since 1992, back when shoulder pads became unisex. In 2020, largely in response to Trump's crazy antics, we had six women presidential candidates—one day we'll make history, and sis, once we go there, we'll never want to go back.

This royal shift also follows on the skirts of the #MeToo movement, where women across industries and courtrooms began clapping back against bad behavior, so, boo-boo, it's pretty much guaranteed that pussy-grabbing presidents won't have it so easy in the future. Eventually the balls will be in the court of women and minorities as they become the majority population, which is expected by 2050, and then we can really figure out how to fix certain systems that get power-hungry, reality-show-making, money-mongering, shady presidents elected in the first place.

Oh, and a note to the political trolls and O'Reillys: do not poke at Auntie Maxine if you're not picking a fight. This sista is one of the warriors, the strong Black women who raise up, and no, bro—*chuckle*—you don't want to mess with that power.

What Auntie Maxine Wants for YOU

I'm very optimistic about your future. I do expect you to do better than the last generation.

I want you to be the leaders that I know that you can be.

I want you to have all of these positions of leadership.

I want you to have a good quality of life. I want you to earn good money, have a great career.

I want you to live well.

I want your children's children to live well.

Some people say, "Well, can we have all of that?"

Ladies and gentlemen, we can have all of that. We deserve that, and you must have it.

—*Maxine Waters, Speech at National Youth Summit, August 9, 2003, Catholic University, Washington, DC*

* * * * * * * ★ * * * * * * *

WOMAN

I'm a strong
Black woman.
I cannot
be intimidated.
I cannot
be undermined.

—MAXINE WATERS, MSNBC

QUEEN OF SLAY

I slay
And I mean to boo from the curls in my
hair to the bottom of my shoes.
—Nia Sioux, feat. Coco Jones, "Slay"

Shortly after high school, Maxine married Edward Waters, and they had two children, Edward Jr. and Karen. Following her husband's stint in the army, the Waters family moved to Los Angeles in 1960. Eventually, Edward went to work at a printing plant, and Maxine worked in a garment factory downtown. She later worked as a telephone operator for Pacific Telephone and then as a service representative—all a very, very long way from Capitol Hill.

A slice of history would occur and bump up against Maxine's life as a wife and mother, and steer her into activism on August 11, 1965, while she was still working at the garment factory. Watts, a deeply impoverished community (and still one of the most impoverished in Los Angeles) at the time was predominantly African American, having fallen into poverty after the factories and many white residents left the neighborhood. A twenty-one-year-old Black man, Marquette Frye, was driving his mother's 1955 Buick with his brother Ronald in the passenger seat when he was pulled over by a white California Highway Patrolman named Lee W. Minikus on suspicion of driving while intoxicated.

Why the suspicion? Je ne sais pas.

Minikus reportedly administered a sobriety test and arrested Frye, ordering his mother's car to be impounded. Ronald went to get their mother, and she showed up and witnessed an ordeal in which her son was brutally struck and choked, and when she jumped to his defense, she was also struck. A police officer pulled out a shotgun, and another reportedly kicked a pregnant woman. The crowd became enraged by the injustice it was witnessing, and a circle of irrepressible emotion erupted, spreading like wildfire across Avalon Boulevard. More police were sent in, along with their dogs, who roared and pulled at the people. Punches were thrown, and Black bodies fought back hard and boldly for the years of being mistreated, not listened to, and misunderstood.

Watts had once been a thriving community of Black and white working-class people. But still, there had long been racial tension. Discrimination was still showing its merciless face in the housing divide, where in some areas of Los Angeles, Blacks could not rent or buy property, even after doing so was made legal in 1948.

Many of the people who migrated to Los Angeles, both Black and white, had taken a train route that extended from New Orleans, across Mississippi, Alabama, Texas, and Arizona. The last stop on that journey was called Watts Station.

Though their desire had been to get away from the problems of the Deep South, they once again encountered all the same attitudes and prejudices that had made life so difficult there. By 1965, Watts residents were piled into public housing developments, similar to those built in St. Louis—crowded into one community and layered regularly with harassment and social suffocation by police who seemed able to get away with the abuse.

SOMEHOW THE FRYE incident that particular Wednesday made the people of Watts decide enough was enough. They slapped back that ugly hand of bigotry the best they could; anger that day decided to strike down and not pull back. They would not relent. As the rebellion stretched, and spread only farther and wider, brown hands tore down cars, looted and damaged the stores, and created a figure of ruin that reflected their experience as Blacks in America.

A rebellion would make America listen, wouldn't it? James Baldwin once said, "Not everything faced can be changed. But nothing can be changed until it is faced." Whether the rebellion was beneficial depends on the perspective from which your eyes gaze. But it was a strange and confusing time in America, to say the least.

The Watts riots actually occurred just days after President Lyndon B. Johnson had signed the Voting Rights Act of 1965, the law that would make it possible for Maxine Waters to one day become an elected official and a member of Congress.

The act had been the result of civil rights activism by the Student Nonviolent Coordinating Committee (SNCC) chaired by John Lewis, and the Southern Christian Leadership Conference (SCLC) founded by Martin Luther King Jr. In Selma, Alabama, police engaged in the brutal attack of nonviolent protesters on the Edmund Pettus Bridge. The conflict was broadcast all across the country. Americans could not abide police attacking nonviolent protesters, and with such brutality. The outrage fueled a voting-rights bill that was passed through the House and Senate and signed into law on August 6, 1965.

The 1960s had begun the work of desegregation. Public signs that had separated whites and coloreds had come down. Boundaries that had separated the races were made illegal, as were barriers to voting that had, in the past, effectively nullified the Fourteenth Amendment, which had granted African Americans the right to vote after the Civil War. The Civil Rights Movement had involved strategic legal actions that demonstrated the collective ability of African Americans to become full participants in our democracy. Beyond that, the orderly, peaceful, yet powerful confrontation staged by many different organized groups had demonstrated the dignity and resolve of African Americans. Young white college students flooded to the South to participate in the Mississippi Freedom Summer where, just the year before, three civil rights workers were killed.

But despite these advances, Los Angeles remained troubled. Ninety-five percent of Los Angeles was off limits to Black citizens. They were effectively segregated in Watts. The population of Blacks there grew from 4 percent to 14 percent, from 63,700 in 1940 to 350,000 in 1965.

As job opportunities in factories moved much of the white working class to other places in the city, the African Americans of Watts were stranded. Jobs and services left and these citizens had few places to turn. On August 11, that long day waxed into night and the unrest eventually lasted five days as people came out fighting and took out their rage on a society that had pushed them into a corner.

The LAPD chief, William H. Parker, the man at the helm of the police violence, was well known for his bigoted tactics, such as recruiting officers from the South who held anti-Black sentiments. Parker asked the governor to call in the California National Guard, and at first, two thousand, then sixteen thousand soldiers showed up in Watts, ready to put a stop to the rebellion.

Blood and fear swept the city for days as the battle persisted. Brown bodies guarded fire departments so they could not be water-hosed out. Thirty-four people were reported dead, twenty-three of them killed by law enforcement. Four thousand people were arrested.

It cost so many people everything, but in the moment it was worth it. Blacks were discontented with employment rates, substandard housing, and inadequate schools in Watts and around the country. Something needed to change.

And this is where the queen stepped in.

The Watts rebellion made it plain: Black people were "sick and tired of being sick and tired," Waters said, quoting Fannie Lou Hamer. Blacks had been fighting the daily occurrences of racism's lawless nature their entire lives—Watts was another wave of fire that would inspire stronger civic action and uprising for many.

The queen was now a young mother, pacing the floor and fuming, like every other Black mother, about the police's sickening treatment of the brothas and sistas in Watts. It was no coincidence that a year later, a friend would call up Maxine to tell her about a local ad that was advertising a position in the Watts area to work as an assistant teacher in Head Start.

Head Start was a new federal program aimed at preparing

low-income preschool kids for elementary school, an initiative of President Lyndon Johnson's War on Poverty, aimed at eradicating poverty in the United States. This was just the kind of opportunity Maxine was looking for, and she was all in. As a congresswoman, Auntie Maxine would later say in a statement on the floor in 2010, in remembrance of Jule Sugarman, the founder of the Head Start Program:

> *I can unequivocally say that Head Start changed my life and turned it in a new direction.*
>
> *I vividly remember working as a service representative for the Pacific Telephone Company in Los Angeles in the mid 1960s, and getting excited over a newspaper advertisement I saw for the new Head Start Program. They were seeking staff for this initiative, which would be run by Sargent Shriver out of the Office of Economic Opportunity. Being a mother of young children, and seeking a career path where I could help people and make a difference—despite not having official teaching credentials—I eagerly applied to be an assistant teacher.*
>
> *To my surprise and delight, I was hired as a Head Start assistant teacher. In Los Angeles County the Head Start Program worked closely with community nonprofit groups like the International Federation for Settlements and Neighborhood Centers, so I worked with great people who were truly committed to putting children on a solid path to an*

education, combating poverty, and making our communi-
ties a safer, better place to live.

Head Start encouraged me to finish my education;
taught me the importance and value of community orga-
nizing; made me acutely aware of the many issues facing
our young children; and inspired me to get involved in poli-
tics to make a difference in the lives of others, particularly
the least of these.

Johnson's War on Poverty programs included the Social
Security Amendment of 1965, resulting in the creation of
Medicare and Medicaid; the Food Stamp Act of 1964, which
applied federal resources to alleviate hunger in poor communities; the Economic Opportunity Act of 1964, which offered education and training to cities and states; and the
Elementary and Secondary Education Act, considered to
have the most far-reaching impact on education of any legislation ever passed by Congress. It authorized the disbursement of federal resources to offer professional training for
teachers, the purchase of instructional materials, volunteer
involvement, and more. Many of these programs are still in
existence today, including Head Start, though they are under
attack by groups who would rather federal dollars be dis-
bursed to the rich through tax cuts, entitlements, and subsi-
dies than be used to uplift the working and middle class and
support the prosperity of everyday people. Back in the 1960s,

as a woman coming into her own, Maxine Waters was ready and eager to be part of what was then a new and exciting moment in Black lives.

Maxine and the queens in her community at Head Start thrived throughout the early years of the program. In an interview in the *Los Angeles Times*, she said, "It was exciting, exciting, exciting. At that point in my life I really began to examine where I was and what I really believed in."

Auntie Maxine had finally found a place to plant her power and love for the community. She put on the figurative crown and cape that all the Earth's queens possess, and went soaring into activism to help the children. She knew exactly what sort of help their parents needed, because she was a mother, too, and a woman who had also sprouted from poverty. She knew exactly how to approach them, because she had seen women form a helping army around her mother for years that allowed her to succeed. Like her mom, many of the women in the program had little education or were so busy working and providing that they barely had the bandwidth to get their children prepared and off to school.

Inspired by her past, Maxine would help them in the spirit of Ms. Carter and Ms. Stokes. She took responsibility for these women and their babies; she and the other workers at Head Start offered the children hot meals as well as a curriculum and instruction that would give them a sound start in their education: to ensure they knew the alphabet, how to count, were socialized with the discipline to operate in a classroom environment, and could interact with other children without conflict or anxiety, and would foster other academic and social aspects of readiness. Head Start was a program that could give low-income children the same opportunity to succeed in school that financially privileged kids had. This is what Maxine Waters, a girl from the St. Louis projects, wanted for them.

The Watts rebellion, the biggest insurrection ever to occur in Los Angeles history, happened because many African Americans were suffering under the brutality of the LAPD, racism, and segregation. Waters and the Head Start team knew that if they helped children become ready to learn, it would begin to "level the playing field," as she'd say, so that all children had an equal opportunity to succeed. Then they would have the tools to fight against the injustice that had caused the riots in the first place.

One of Maxine's jobs as the supervisor of parent involvement and volunteer services was to coordinate community volunteers, giving them an invitation to join in community activism. "Not only did we teach parents that they could take control of their children's educational destiny but we also taught them the value of interacting with elected officials and the school board, and how they could manage and take control of their communities. We encouraged them to contact public officials for federal budget requests for increased funding. And of course I was learning all the while, and this was a real defining moment for me."

By creating bonds with those women volunteers, Maxine was unknowingly building a sturdy network. *Shoot*, that #momlife can be powerful in building an army, and Head Start was a good place to form a base. These women would voluntarily ride or die for the cause—the B-hive, Little Monsters, Arianators, Youngbloods, or Avocados have nothing on mom power. Maxine was beginning to apply her natural bent toward advocacy, and her *she* tribe would only get stronger. In this role, she learned about the power of government and discovered how to push and pull levers to make things happen for them. She developed an on-the-ground understanding of politics' role in equity and how by making it a focus of her activism she could get assistance that would directly help improve the lives of those in her community.

Yes, sis, the Head Start in Watts was the beginning of Waters's activism, and she decided the next step was completing higher education for herself. She enrolled in California State University, Los Angeles, and by 1970 she had earned her bachelor's degree in sociology.

MAXINE WATERS WENT where her heart led her, and her next steps would take her from the boardrooms of social work in Head Start to politics. This transition would be both tumultuous and smooth for Waters, because she wasn't climbing Capitol Hill for the status. Her mission had to do with matters of the heart, her core belief in what was right, and the power Ma Dear had instilled in her to fight. She once told the *Huffington Post*, "I truly believe in justice. And I truly believe in equality. And one of the things that I really did like in seventh and eighth grade was the Constitution. And I believe in it, I believe in people, I believe that everybody deserves the opportunity to have a decent quality of life. I believe that discrimination is intolerable. I believe that injustice and inequality must be fought against all the time."

Maxine was also getting excited about the Black electoral candidates surfacing. As she began to take in the mighty role that politics could play in reshaping society, both as an employee of a federal initiative and as an advocate and activist, she began volunteering in political campaigns. She volunteered for Mervyn M. Dymally (the first African American to serve in the California State Senate, and who ultimately was elected to Congress); Mayor Tom Bradley (the first and only African American mayor of Los Angeles, as of this writing); and Sen. Alan Cranston. She knocked on doors in the district, stuffed envelopes, and designed brochures with great pride and excitement about what was possible for the future, and the contribution that she as a Black woman in the community could make.

In 1972, Maxine divorced Edward Waters. Her passion for

organizing and community service began to eclipse the hours she could spend tending to her marriage. She and her husband drifted apart and finally they divorced. Waters continued on her career path as a solo mom. She had discovered something burning inside her, and it was a fire that would not burn out. She had found a way that she could really help. She had found systematic ways to make a difference in people's lives. But she was beginning to realize that there was also something bigger and more pervasive happening, something that reached all the way to the White House and the halls of Capitol Hill.

But homegirl still had to make a living and pay the bills. She had grown as a professional. More important, she could now see in her eyes the reflections of a leader. As opportunities opened up for Black professionals, a professional class began to emerge. There were Black athletes, entertainers, corporate officers, cosmetics companies, magazine publishers, radio stations, and all kinds of business; Waters's contact list began to grow into many different markets.

So she started a business, engaging in a short stint of entrepreneurship when she opened a public relations firm with her partner John Floyd. It was called Floyd Waters. It was an exciting endeavor, and was another milestone that showed anything was possible for Maxine Waters from St. Louis. "We didn't know anything about access to capital," she told *Essence*. "We really started out of our pockets. We had to maintain our office, and we had one person, a receptionist, working for us. John and I did everything." Yet they had successes, like handling the PR for the film *Sounder*, starring Cicely Tyson. During an era of Blaxploitation films, like *Super Fly* and *Shaft*, the film *Sounder* was one of the few family movies that showed a wholesome Black family.

Floyd Waters also managed David S. Cunningham's campaign for city council in 1973. A PR firm handling Black actors as well as politicians definitely had merit, especially when Hollywood and independent Black filmmakers were experiencing a kind of heyday. *Essence* magazine had just begun publication two years earlier. Black radio was at its height and more television opportunities were beginning to open up for Blacks. That year the classic Black sitcom *Sanford and Son* came on the air, and others like *Good Times* and *The Jeffersons* would soon follow. The Congressional Black Caucus was forming and there was even a Black woman member of Congress from California, Yvonne Brathwaite Burke.

It was all starting to come together—when Cunningham won, he quickly realized that this Maxine Waters was obviously a *boss*, and he needed her smarts and willpower all to himself. He invited her to join him as his chief deputy. *Boom!* The queen had planted a foot in the chamber, making her one of the highest-ranking Black women in city hall.

And this was just the beginning.

THE ROSE THAT GREW FROM CONCRETE

I'm free to be the greatest,
I'm alive.
—Sia, feat. Kendrick Lamar, "The Greatest"

Yaasss, girlfriend, in 1973, as chief deputy to David Cunningham in the city council, Maxine Waters wore her crown equally in politics and activism. In fact, Auntie Maxine would stay true to these mixed roots, unlike many politicians, and has never felt the need to separate the two. She once told the *Washington Post*, "I believe in protest. I believe in organizing power to resist discrimination, resist racism, resist womanizing—all of that. I'm an activist legislator."

She had learned how to run a successful campaign and now was an official player in Democratic politics. *Whoop-whoop*, ladies, the future was shining bright for Ms. Maxine Waters! So much so, our girl was glowing, *okay!*

Recognizing that light and Auntie Maxine's natural gift for leadership, women started suggesting that she run for public office, because, you know, queens see queens. And we lift each other up: Rachel and Monica, Molly and Issa, Celie and Nettie. Maxine began to get involved with organizations related to the women's movement, such as the National Organization for Women (NOW) and the National Women's Political Caucus (NWPC), and received their support too. She began working with women like Gloria Steinem, one of the founders of *Ms.* magazine, and Bella Abzug, a lawyer and activist, who later became a congresswoman from New York, early in the movement when women were coming forth, candid and discerning about their intentions to run for office as women for women's rights. "Gloria asked me to serve on the board of the Ms. Foundation [for Women], where I was able to see all of the unsolicited proposals that came in—from women in coal-mining country, women needing places to go to be sheltered from domestic violence. Of course, it was not only eye-opening, it was the kind of learning experience that helped me to be a better public policymaker."

And then just when an idea sparks, and what was once a dream or aspiration now seems to have legs and walks in front of you leading the way, ye sister, this was happening for Maxine Waters—now she was running for State Assembly!

In 1976, 48th District State Assembly Member Leon Ralph left office to accept a calling to the ministry. This district represented a portion of South Central and portions of areas like Lynwood and South Gate—areas that largely served people of color. However, just before leaving his seat Ralph endorsed his young aide, Johnny Collins, who suddenly filed for the post the day before the deadline, effectively closing the door on any possibility of competition. But Waters and the women behind her *Were. Not. Having. It.*

Repeat: *Were. Not. Having. It.*

Waters and her crew marched right over to Secretary of State March Fong Eu and the ACLU and protested what had been done, and they demanded an opportunity; Eu reopened the filing for another five days.

Collins had certain advantages over Waters due to the endorsement of the incumbent and the financial and organizational resources that came with it—**yawn**. *What?* There was nothing to worry about here. Sis, Waters had us—a nonconforming she army, a not-so-secret, not-so-quiet weapon that could destroy Collins and that made her a very strong counter for bruh; she had a movement behind her, the sheroes! Women warriors like Margaret Wright and Mary Henry stood by her side.

In a show of solidarity as feminists, they knocked on doors all across the district. Waters even had white women on the west side of Los Angeles come out to help her. Although she had white feminist allies working alongside her, she took the words of Black women very seriously. In many ways, Black women's voices had historically been considered a second-tier in the feminist movement, even overlooked by

those allies with the best intentions, but for Maxine Waters their perspective mattered more than anything, and they had her ear. The women's movement had begun to unleash the ambition of all women who wanted to do more than stay home and raise children. Black women began to see themselves as leaders, as activists, as participants in a struggle, and they were believing in their power to change things. In fact, their words were the words of her campaign. "Why not? Why not a woman?" they'd say. "It's time."

And she used those words to run. By using their voices she was doing something completely unheard of.

She also clearly understood the differences between the Black feminists and white feminists, and was able to hear both. Years later, on *On One with Angela Rye*, she explained it:

Black women, for example, didn't talk about abortions. Whatever happened with midwives was not to be talked about. White women were very vocal and open about it. They had buttons with a hanger on it that said "I had one." Black women didn't talk about freedom of choice in the way that white women did. Sometimes that caused some people to say there was a real difference between Black and white women [feminists]. However we did have Black women who were real feminists, and who gave leadership to the feminist movement. Even though issues were talked about differently and people showed up differently, there was a strong belief from all women—Black and white—that something was wrong with our society that didn't treat women equally and didn't give women equal opportunities.

Waters and her army devised an unusual campaign strategy that set her apart. "The community that I was running for still had a lot of white conservatives. We had to find ways to talk to them, to add to the minority side," she told Rye. At the time gardens were becoming a big thing, and they chose a unique PR strategy that played on the fact that people were becoming more and more passionate about growing their own food. The campaign began mailing packets of vegetable and fruit seeds to potential voters. (Often under the gaze of the onlooking postal workers, who enjoyed the sudden parade of strong women coming in and out, she later told Angela Rye. *wink*) They ordered a twenty-five-pound sack of seeds and little envelopes. "At the time, the community was basically a still-growing Latino population, more Black population, and a dying-out white population. We sent carrot seeds to the whites, we sent cilantro to the Mexicans, and collard greens to the Blacks. We would go knocking on doors . . . Years later, because collard green stalks grow real tall with big leaves, and they stay for years, people would tell me, 'Come see my stalk,' or 'I'm gonna fix you some collard greens,' and on and on."

The mailing of the seeds allowed Maxine and her feminist

supporters to tie her candidacy to something memorable that voters would not likely forget. And it worked!

But her volunteers were also met with the same stubborn prejudices that, even today, still characterize parts of Southern California politics. But her white, feminist supporters took care of that. "One of my friends who was working from NWPC knocked on a door, responded to by a white male, and she asked him if he would vote for this woman named Maxine Waters—they didn't have my picture. So he said, 'Is she a . . . n-word?' And she said, 'No, she's a woman,' and he said, 'OK!'"

Auntie Maxine also aligned herself with the right people in power, to give herself that extra dose of influence that always helps a campaign. She sought the endorsement of Mayor Tom Bradley, who before becoming the first Black mayor of Los Angeles in 1973 had represented the nearby 10th District. Our girl helped him in numerous ways when she worked as a city councilman's chief deputy, as well as during his campaigns, but he, for some reason, decided he could not endorse her. At that point, Waters's campaign was bleeding cash and barely surviving on loans from supporters—Cunningham gave her $17,500, which helped pay some bills, but she needed a push to get her over the top. If she didn't have the funds, she would go hard for securing the best connections. Assembly elections are often quieter, and less funded, than other popular elections, so endorsements are key.

Tom Bradley wasn't coming through, so the queen contemplated what to do.

And once again, it would be a woman who gave her the push and support that she needed.

Ethel Bradley, Tom Bradley's wife but also a co-founder with Waters of the Black Women's Forum, gave Waters her own endorsement instead. Yoncé, these women did not come to play, they came to *slay*. Besides her clout as a powerful mayor's wife, Bradley also organized more supporters for Waters's campaign, including Las Angelenas who could bring out the Latino vote.

This was Waters's first race, and she'd win over and over again, but even in the early years Auntie Maxine was a fierce lioness on the campaign trail capable of hunting down the win. She knew how to bring the drama to get the best results. Not only does this bae dress to the nines, but she's an avid runner and swimmer, and any of her competitors should expect a political ass-kicking with the force of a triathlete. It wasn't surprising to her team when one day she made a bold strategic move by flying 2,300 miles to Washington, DC, to get a photograph.

The photo was to be with US senator Hubert Humphrey, who had been President Johnson's vice president. Later, after losing his own campaign for the presidency, Humphrey returned to the Senate representing the state of Minnesota. Humphrey won respect in his own right for the Humphrey–

Hawkins bill that sought to strike at the core of unemployment in American communities. Auntie Maxine knew a photo with Humphrey could make all the difference and could serve as a tangible symbol of her acceptance by a high-profile Democrat, and she felt that it was key for her campaign. For a queen on a mission, miles fall beneath the wind of her cape and time will stand still, if needed. Auntie Maxine would go to meet him face-to-face.

She arrived in DC, grabbed a photographer from the gaggle of reporters that huddle trying to get interviews with members of Congress outside the Senate chambers. When Humphrey walked off the floor into the hallway, she caught him and explained what she was doing. He said OK, and she got the photo. She turned right back around, got on the next flight to L.A., and her team quickly printed a brochure with the photo on the cover. The women sent it out everywhere, near and far, all over the land. The queen was aligned with the cause, and—ta-da!—once again Auntie Maxine's strategy worked!

She won with 48.2 percent of the vote, and in 160 of the 201 precincts. *Hurrah!*

Maxine Waters became a member of the California Assembly and would serve for the next fourteen years. *Yesss!*

Auntie Maxine's Memo

TO THE <u>MISOGYNIST</u> IN YOUR LIFE

★ "Keep your nasty comments away from us, keep your tricks and your lies to yourself, and keep your hands off our backs and our goddamn bodies."

★ "We're waging our own war against rape and sexual harassment. We're waging a war against the perverts who believe we can be misused or exploited in the interests of a job, or recognition, or even so-called love."

★ Regarding Trump: "Just remember what Hillary should have said: 'Creep, get off my back!'"

—Excerpt from Women's Convention speech,
Saturday, October 28, 2017

BLACK LOVE

Your love is King
Crown you with my heart.
—Sade, "Your Love Is King"

round the time Maxine's career was taking off, she began dating a tall, dark, handsome **wink** and notably, *ooooh* slightly younger man named Sidney Williams, a former NFL player. **wink, wink**

Sidney was born on March 24, 1942, in Shreveport, Louisiana, but was raised in Houston, Texas, where he lived most of his life before graduating from Phillis Wheatley High School and Southern University in Baton Rouge. He's a Kappa, ladies, a member of the fraternity Kappa Alpha Psi. All this to say, we see why Auntie Maxine was feelin' Sid.

More important, it was what they had in common beneath the surface that made her smitten with him. His motivations were equally set on being one of the best linebackers in the NFL and being a strong role model and change agent in the Black community. Sidney was the linebacker on two NFL championship teams: the Cleveland Browns and the Balti-more Colts. He also played for a year with the Washington Redskins and the Pittsburgh Steelers. While he was playing in the NFL, he attended a news conference with other athletes who stood alongside heavyweight champion Muhammad Ali when he refused to be drafted into the US military for religious reasons. Ali was convicted of draft evasion, banned from the sport of boxing for three years, fined, and stripped of his title. And you thought Colin Kaepernick was committed?

In addition to being an athlete, Williams served in the National Guard on both active duty and reserve.

If that résumé isn't sexy enough, he was also politically minded, and that's how he met his queen. While Maxine was chief of staff for Cunningham, Sid worked in his office as well, and he must have caught her eye across the way in the office. *wink*

At six-foot-two, dear Sidney has a handsome and calming presence about him, sort of like Sidney Poitier. While Auntie Maxine was all wide smile and flamboyant personality, he gave off a sturdy steadiness beside her. They were a handsome chocolate pair, to say the least, but best of all he shared in her greatest passions, to use politics as activism and improve the life of the Black community. So, sis, you can imagine the luscious romance of these two's initial dates, softly whispering about Black love, revolution, and legislation under moonlit skies.

They were married in 1977, and he became Edward and Karen's stepfather.

As time passed, he developed into a businessman and philanthropist. He was a project manager for the Los Angeles Community Redevelopment Agency, and then for some time he went to work as a Mercedes-Benz salesman in Hollywood from 1979 to 1994. During this time, he also worked with Pro Football Hall of Famer Jim Brown on the Black Economic Union, an organization Brown started to help minority-owned businesses. The organization's motto was "Produce, Achieve, and Prosper." They opened offices around the country and received financial support from the Ford Foundation to help their efforts. According to Brown, they started more than four hundred businesses around the country that were owned and operated by African Americans.

Later, he was appointed US ambassador to the Bahamas by President Bill Clinton. Sidney is a *cat* who has lived many lives. Lady Maxine had finally found her guy.

★ ★ ★ ★ ★ ★ ★ ★ ★ ★ ★ ★ ★ ★

LEADER

I didn't create an image for myself. I'm just me and I won't change.

—MAXINE WATERS, INTERVIEW WITH MARK GLADSTONE, *LOS ANGELES TIMES*

"WE'RE NOT MEN"

We gave you life, we gave you birth . . .
We fem the future, don't make it worse.
—Janelle Monáe, "Django Jane"

Maxine's first order of business when she was elected to the California State Assembly was to correct her title: *Assemblyman.* Okaayyy. As a feminist, imagine how she squirmed when they kept referring to her as such. And gurl, on her day one in office, Auntie Maxine stepped in ready to put up a fight about it. The first bill she authored was to have the official address for members of the assembly changed from "Assemblyman" to "Assemblyperson" or "Assemblymember."

"I didn't know I was going to create such a stir," she told Rye. "The men went crazy. They said I was trying to neuter them. They were really taken aback by this new member who was going to come and change the language . . . so they took me on."

Fortunately, she had an influential friend named Willie

Brown, who had served on the California State Assembly and would become Speaker, a post he held for fifteen years, and the first African American mayor of San Francisco. "I remember the first day I was in the assembly and I tried to take on the entire body, and not have them refer to us as assemblymen. I thought the women needed to be called assemblymember, and of course, all of those legislators took me on and they slashed into me, and Willie Brown came to my defense. He jumped up on the floor and said that he was my attorney representing me," Waters shared, clearly tickled by that, in the 1993 *Willie Brown* documentary, "and he defended me at a time when I didn't know what to do under attack. . . . He allowed me and many others an opportunity to realize our potential, by giving us assignments and letting us excel in ways that we wanted to. . . . I was proud that I helped to make Willie Brown Speaker."

DURING HER FOURTEEN-YEAR tenure in California state politics, Waters gained national and international attention for her outspoken, no-holds-barred style but also for many of her legislative efforts. One of her proudest was, in 1984, when she joined a powerful coalition of Black political executives who founded the Free South Africa movement. Randall Robinson, a Harvard-trained lawyer, was the founder of TransAfrica (and brother to the first Black network news anchor on television, Max Robinson). Robinson brought with him the chair of the US Civil Rights Commission, Mary Frances Berry; US Delegate from Washington, DC, Walter Fauntroy; and Eleanor Holmes Norton, then a Yale-trained lawyer and professor at Georgetown University. All of these people were accomplished and admired in their time, and all of them had cut their teeth in some way in the struggles for equal justice in America. TransAfrica was headquartered in DC, and Waters joined the coalition determined to create a Los Angeles branch.

One of TransAfrica's initiatives was to create American public awareness of the struggle in South Africa by engaging in civil disobedience. This would shift American foreign policy in South Africa to one of constructive engagement, which would incentivize South Africa to confront its systemic racial problems and have their activism influence other Western nations to follow suit. It would also put pressure on American interests to divest their support in South Africa and end the apartheid regime that had imprisoned Nelson Mandela and continuously terrorized his wife, Winnie Mandela, and their family. These ideas came directly out of the intellectual and philosophical arguments of the civil rights movement, which had asserted the need for Black unity across the peoples of the African diaspora. During this time, African Americans could be seen wearing traditional or stylized African garments made out of African prints and cloth as a display of African unity. More natural hairdos emerged, and bold patterns and flamboyant color took over the Black fashion scene.

The coalition planned and executed repeated sit-ins in front of the embassy of South Africa in Washington, DC, and regularly staged protests where marchers were arrested and taken to jail. While 4,500 protesters were arrested in one year, the Free South Africa Movement (FSAM) was also pushing universities and American businesses to divest their holdings in South Africa. Waters devised a goal to advocate that the state of California divest significant holdings in the South African diamond business and curtail its interaction with the South African government.

Then, in 1980, after serving on the Democratic National Committee, Waters began to lead sit-ins, marches, and rallies against corporations doing business with South Africa's apartheid regime, and successfully authored legislation that constituted the largest divestment of state pension funds from businesses with dealings in South Africa. She also authored an assembly bill that called for the divestment of $12 million from the California state pension fund from corporations that were doing business in South Africa. She has led efforts and continues to facilitate congressional agendas to cancel the debts that impoverished countries in Africa and Latin America owe to wealthy institutions like the World Bank and to free poor countries from international debt.

Sis, she was also responsible for landmark affirmative-action legislation that opened state procurement and contracting opportunities to women- and minority-owned businesses.

Many people don't know much about Auntie Maxine's work, but she's been around pulling back the curtain on injustice behind the scenes for a long time. She authored numerous pieces of legislation, including: a law requiring state agencies to award a percentage of public contracts to minorities and women, tenants' rights laws, and a law restricting police officers in their use of strip searches. She created the first statewide child-abuse-prevention training program.

For her tireless efforts to serve and her significant, effective legislative achievements, Waters's capability as a legislator was recognized when she was named chair of the Assembly Democratic Caucus. The chair leads all the Democratic members of the assembly, sets the Democratic agenda for each legislative session, is in charge of persuading members of the caucus to vote for the agenda, and works across the aisle to win votes from Republicans, especially when the Democrats are in the minority, to assure passage of the Democratic agenda, so that bills are signed into law.

By 1985, Waters was focused on establishing effective resources for the community. She created Project Build, a job-training program for unemployed people living in L.A.'s housing projects. At Nickerson Gardens, one of the housing projects where the program was launched, 1,500 out of

4,000 residents were unemployed at the time. Nickerson consists of 156 buildings with town house–style units joined to single-bedroom units. The community was almost 95 percent African American, and some call it the birthplace of the Bloods.

Thanks to Auntie Maxine's advocacy, the state Employment Development Department provided $250,000 in funding for the program. Auntie Maxine and the job experts whom she enlisted from the area created the workshop's content. The seminars instructed the residents on how to fill out a job application, how to interview, and how to find childcare. On the last day, major employers at the time like Unocal, Charles Drew Postgraduate Medical School, and Pacific Bell, where Waters herself had been employed, would come to interview the residents. If the residents attended all four classes, they would attend a graduation ceremony. The classes served up to one hundred participants. Auntie Maxine was so committed that she would conduct some of the four-day seminars herself. Many of the students were welfare recipients or students lacking a high school diploma who had given up on the job search. But they just needed a spark of encouragement, and that spark was Maxine Waters. Some of the graduates ended up getting jobs and others went on to get their high school diploma or professional training. And the program didn't leave the others behind, either—there were always follow-up sessions with counselors if they weren't able to find a job the first time.

The Maxine Waters Employment Preparation Center (MWEPC) was established in 1989, an official school within the Los Angeles Unified School District (LAUSD). It had formerly been the Watts Skills Center. The center offered vocational education in areas such as nursing, banking, and auto mechanics, and was named after the assemblywoman for the work she had blessed upon the community.

Read: Auntie Maxine is much, much more than a meme, baby. *snap, snap*

★

DEAR FRIEND, IT'S LONELY UP HERE

You are what you choose to be.
It's not up to no one else.
—Kehlani, "Bright"

Assemblywoman Maxine Waters was winning. But even after fourteen years of work in the assembly, there was still work to do. Work only a queen could do.

It started with a campaign letter written from a fellow Black unicorn. The unicorn revealed that she was lonely. She had worked hard to get to the castle, but like many other women, after much climbing and succeeding to leave her stamp at the peak, in the nook of the glass ceiling, she turned around and realized she was alone on the throne. That unicorn was Rep. Cardiss Collins, the fourth African American woman in Congress.

Rep. Cardiss Collins of Illinois, the first African American woman to represent any Midwestern state in Congress, had joined the US House of Representatives when her husband,

George, was killed in the crash of United Airlines Flight 553 in December 1972. At the time of her husband's death, there was only one other Black woman in the House, the first Black female member of Congress, Shirley Chisholm of New York. There were a few other white women members to follow, all newly elected—Ella Grasso of Connecticut; Louise Day Hicks of Massachusetts, Elizabeth Andrews (who also succeeded her husband) from Alabama; Margaret Heckler, a Republican from Massachusetts; and Patsy Mink of Hawaii. All of these women were just finding their way around the House, but they wanted more. They wanted to engage new voices, so Collins became part of a campaign organized by women's groups to encourage others to run. And Maxine Waters heard that call.

Collins felt powerful in her position to create change. She'd been shy and a bit intimidated during her first days on the Hill as the brown-hued lady in a mostly white canvas cracking at the edges with a lot of testosterone. But she'd overcome that, and now she was firm and assertive, with a sophisticated clap back, but there was one major thing that bothered her, nagged at her continuously, actually.

"Dear Friend," she wrote in the letter, "it's lonely up here."

And a tribe of rebel women followed.

One by one they appeared. Maxine Waters. Barbara-Rose Collins. Eleanor Holmes Norton. It was 1976; these women were among the many, from Los Angeles to Detroit, and all around the nation, who picked up the baton and ran for election that year and surged into the largest Black female congressional delegation since the 1968 election of the first Black woman representative, Shirley Chisholm. *Yaasss. *clapping**

Black women were marginalized in Congress for years, even in the Congressional Black Caucus, and Collins wanted to create a movement steeped in Shirley Chisholm's famous words, "If they don't give you a seat at the table, demand it," which beckoned Auntie Maxine and other queens for years to come to take up their thrones.

The election of 1972 had been another watershed moment for women in politics. Bella Abzug (NY), Elizabeth Holtzman (NY), Yvonne Brathwaite Burke (CA), Barbara Jordan (TX), Pat Schroeder (CO), Lindy Boggs (LA), and Marjorie Holt, a Republican from Maryland, were all elected to Congress. Maxine may have wanted to run, but she would have to wait until there was an opportunity.

AS REP. COLLINS called for more Black women beside her in Congress, the opportunity for Maxine Waters to join her presented itself when Augustus "Gus" F. Hawkins, a founding member of the Congressional Black Caucus, retired. Maxine Waters ran for the 29th District (which became the 35th District in 1992 and then the 43rd District in 2012) that same year in 1976.

She had become a political star, sis, and was expected to become Hawkins's heir. *Hurrah!* Our girl had come a *looong* way since those days eating in the basement of Thompson's restaurant. The entire nation had as well.

Waters had a regular campaign trail and schedule, visiting churches and local ogranizations, but of course there were haters. Some folks wanted to see her sweat more, work for it. The media complained and were horrified that it looked so easy for this Maxine Waters lady. But that's just what #slaypower looks like, effortless. She had worked hard to get where she was. She now raised hundreds of thousands of dollars for her campaign easily, due to her rising public profile and successes as a leader in the assembly, while her opponents couldn't even get close enough to touch her game. They were invisible beside the queen's shining star. *Um, what were their names again?* Her opponents, Republican Bill De-Witt and Libertarian Waheed R. Boctor, really had no chance of winning. They were up against Maxine Waters, ha! And oh yeah, the district's registered Democrats outnumbered Republicans by 7 to 1.

As everyone expected, Waters won, and was elected to California's 29th Congressional District. She won with more than 79 percent of the popular vote.

By the time Waters got to the House of Representatives, nineteen women had gone before her. Some notable ones were among those she had admired and would finally have a chance to work with—Geraldine Ferraro (NY), who would become the first woman vice presidential nominee; Barbara Boxer (CA); Barbara Mikulski (MD); Gladys Spellman (MD); Mary Rose Oakar (OH); Louise Slaughter (NY); and Nita Lowey (NY).

The three Black women elected with Waters would be new voices for the voiceless: Barbara-Rose Collins in Motown Michigan's 13th District; Eva Clayton of the 1st District of North Carolina, who'd supported her children while working three jobs and with help from food stamps and public medical benefits; and Eleanor Holmes Norton of DC, who had been an instrumental support to Bayard Rustin during the March on Washington and was a member of the DC branch of the SNCC. Norton, a Yale Law School graduate, had clerked for the legendary Black district court judge A. Leon Higginbotham Jr., and had become a civil rights lawyer with the American Civil Liberties Union. Mayor John Lindsay of New York appointed Norton to head the city's Human Rights Commission, and she held the first hearings in the country on discrimination against women. Norton is still a member of Congress today.

WATERS WAS KNOWN for her unapologetic edge and clap back when warranted. Many of Waters's soon-to-be new colleagues purred and whined, Oh, is she fit for Congress? Oh,

is she going to correct her attitude now? Oh, I'm scared of everything and hold me. Oh, oh, oh. They worried that she was leaving an assembly of only 80 members for the big House to be one among 435 members. Could she handle it? Would she be so special then?, they wondered, or, rather, gossiped. She'd be a small fish swimming in a large pond now. The news pundits pondered whether she could roll with the big fish.

They obviously did not know Auntie Maxine.

A queen does not conform to what others think of her.

For generation after generation, honey—historically, traditionally, politically, socially, physically—women, but especially those like Maxine Waters, aka Black, were told to hush up and back down from showing up and especially with a sense of authority. When Auntie Maxine arrived, she wasn't going to take the sugar out of the Kool-Aid for anyone. Like all the Queens of the Resistance, she's outspoken because she must be; it's a necessity. Congress wasn't going to be her Kryptonite. They would have to strap on helmets or protective wear if they were so afraid, because hell yes, the queen was coming. And history would prove wrong the haters and doubters about whether she belonged there.

Auntie Maxine's entrance into Congress in 1990 came at an auspicious time, because the country had reached another heated turning point. Just two months after Maxine's inauguration, the new congresswoman was traveling on business when she saw horrifying news footage from her hotel room. Incredible events were unfolding in Los Angeles. She stared from her bed as the TV showed Rodney King, a construction worker, and his two friends, Bryant Allen and Freddie Helms. The three had been riding in a car in the San Fernando Valley on the 210 freeway when they were stopped by the police. The police demanded that all the men get out of the car and lie facedown on the pavement. Allen said that while he was lying on the ground he was kicked, stomped, taunted, and threatened. King was slow to emerge from the vehicle, and when he did he was told to get on the ground, at which point five police officers surround him on all sides and begin brutally beating him with nightsticks. A civilian filmed the incident and sent the footage to a local news station. Although this was before the days of cell phone cameras, the tragic video was shared rapidly around the country.

Like most of America, Auntie Maxine was outraged.

She immediately hopped on a flight back to L.A.

Tensions were high and hot, but they quickly boiled over when an all-white jury acquitted the officers charged in the beating. Many in the nation were once again shocked, traumatized, and emotionally scarred. It was unbelievable. Any calm the hearing had provided turned into wild outrage that immediately went from *zero to one hundred*. Within hours, the city was choked and ablaze, and many lives turned upside down.

Certain areas of the city had to be completely vacated,

families had to seek public shelter, and businesses were looted and set on fire. By the time Auntie Maxine got back to L.A., the city had turned the water off and the streetlights out, and with their trauma the residents were walking in the dark.

Auntie Maxine responded like a paramedic. She had been through this before during the 1965 Watts riots, and she was angry all over again. Instead of running for cover, she rushed straight to her district. She didn't stop at government offices or police precincts; she went straight to the housing projects. She held meetings with the residents and asked them what they needed. Stores were shuttered and deserted. She thought of the children without food, diapers, and milk as the stores burned down, and she ran around collecting supplies to get back to the residents. She then went into the offices and demanded that the electricity and water be turned back on again in South Central.

And she called the Rev. Jesse Jackson. She wanted to know *right now* how they could begin to file civil-rights charges against the city of Los Angeles and against the acquitted cops.

Auntie Maxine was also furious about how the media was depicting the community. They were painted as a slum of thugs and thieves. Acquitted? Auntie Maxine understood their anger. She knew the truth. A pain had been released onto the streets. These flowers were withered and tired from injustice.

When the mayor, Tom Bradley, called the response to the acquittal a "riot," Auntie Maxine clapped back and told him to curb his language. It was not a riot, it was an "insurrection."

Weeks before Tom Bradley's comments, Auntie Maxine had written an impassioned letter, published in the *Los Angeles Times* on April 14, 1993, validating the people's anger and frustration, but kept it *100* like Auntie always does, and urged them to stop the violence:

When the verdicts come down, there will be thousands of police, sheriffs and National Guard on the streets. If you take to the streets with a Molotov cocktail in hand, a gun in your belt or a brick ready to throw, you give the police the legal right to kill you.

Our anger and frustration must not drive us to the streets. We must use our minds and our God-given talents and our legacy of perseverance and struggle. We must fight our battles in the courtroom, and in the halls of power. We must organize and rally and protest. And, through it all, we will celebrate living—not dying.

I wish we could make life better for everyone, today. I wish we all had jobs, and happy, loving experiences each day of our lives. I wish we had peace of mind. And, if I could, I would give it to you.

Each day brings a new opportunity, a new possibility. I love you and will fight for you. I need you to stand with me to make this a better place. Let us get smart—it's time to chill!

Soon enough things began to settle down . . . and settle . . . and settle. Until it started to feel like the people had been forgotten. Where was the government? Auntie Maxine's phone was not ringing, there was suddenly just the sound of crickets. The residents rummaged in a demolished community, left to pick up the pieces all by themselves. This was not the American way. When there is war, the government steps in; this had been a kind of a war for their humanity. Auntie Maxine doesn't believe in violence, but when too much time passed after the rebellion without anyone returning her calls, or at least providing a sound strategy on how to rectify the situation, she would make her own insurgence right into the White House. Yes, sis. When President George H. W. Bush invited a group of civil rights leaders to the White House immediately after the rebellion, and she wasn't on the invitation list, she invited herself! To their surprise, she stormed into the room . . . and interrupted. She walked right into that room, neck tight, head held high, with her eye on making a difference.

They gave her a seat at the table.

#BLACKGIRLMAGIC

I'm a wizard, I'm a magician
I do tricks, I'm a school you.
—Chrisette Michele, "Black Girl"

By the time Maxine Waters came to Congress in 1990 a new opposition was mounting, this time from the right side of the aisle, from politicians who unjustly and unfairly deemed human rights and women's rights as mere political correctness. The civil rights struggles of the 1960s, the anti–Vietnam War movement, the women's movement, and a burgeoning gay rights movement, had opponents who resented their advances, and tried to turn them around both in public perception and in the eyes of the law.

After the L.A. Rebellion, when searching for answers, the media tried to pin a lot of the unrest on rap music. But Auntie Maxine is a longtime supporter of rap and rappers, and has always defended its musicians and audience. In fact, in an interview with 105.1's *The Breakfast Club*, she said that she loved Tupac Shakur like a son. When his song "Dear Mama" was topping the charts, she met Tupac at a Mother's Day event. Just like an auntie, she could see past the veneer into the young man he was. "There was a certain sensitivity about him," she said. "I got to know his mom. Tupac for me was very special. He was smart and I loved him."

Tupac's lyrics gave America a clear picture of inner-city struggles, if they would only listen. He was considered a poet and griot of his times. Telling the stories of what so many Black men faced. He was from New York but had become a part of West Coast rap and moved to Los Angeles in 1993. Meanwhile, the media tried to criticize him. "It scares the hell out of people when young Black men get aggressive . . . " Waters told the *Los Angeles Times*. "These are artists with a message and they're forcing America to listen."

So many young men felt that their quiet resistance was never perceived or heard. They made complaints. They tried the normal channels to convey their discontent, but somehow it was only when they reacted according to stereotype that people listened. "It isn't just free speech that we're talking about defending here," Waters continued, "it's a social movement. And that's what people can't stand to confront." She knew young men like Tupac. She felt them. She loved them, and they loved her. She was advocating for them. Defining their lives in terms that the power structure could understand. That's what representatives do, don't they? If they don't, they should. . . .

Auntie Maxine took an aggressive, creative approach to helping to ensure this tumultuous outbreak in L.A. didn't ever happen again. She continuously invited elected officials into South Central so they could get a better understanding of what her constituents faced. She wanted to give them an up-close look at the conditions in South Central communities and hear for themselves what mattered to the residents. There's no better way to do that than having a Black congresswoman walk them through it. She also founded Community Build, a grassroots rebuilding project that helped restore the community after the violence.

WHEN MAXINE WATERS first came to Capitol Hill, Democrats were still in the majority in the House and the Senate. But in the next election, they would lose the majority for the first time in forty years. The House is what is called a "majoritarian" institution—in other words, the majority rules. Whatever the majority says goes, and those in the minority have little power to get things done without pure persuasion, strategic communication, and the creation of shrewd alliances that mutually benefit both parties. This is the primary work of politics, to influence the actions of the federal government in favor of one's constituents, whether your party is in power or out of power. It requires incisive, creative thinking to build alliances, sometimes improbable ones, and to utilize any and every vehicle possible to score a win for one's constituents. At times, when the liberal Democrats were hard to convince, Waters had no problem moving toward the conservative Democrats to find answers for her people.

The country was becoming more conservative and turning a blind eye toward the needs of African Americans. Even though Black social movements had opened up opportunities, conservative Republicans were whipping up resentment against what they termed the "welfare state." President George H. W. Bush had featured a notorious ad during his 1988 campaign, which came to symbolize the vicious, regressive attitude fomented by politicians pointing their fingers at African Americans as the cause of crime, unrest, drugs, and all the ills of American society. The ad was dark and had a menacing tone. It was about a Black man named Willie Horton who had been released from prison on a furlough program and had raped a Maryland woman and stabbed her boyfriend. Bush used the ad against his opponent, Michael Dukakis, a Massachusetts governor who had won his party's nomination, to paint the Democrats as too permissive, too soft on crime, and too afraid to confront the "threat" of Black aggression. The ad, crafted by Republican operative Lee Atwater, helped Bush win the election, but introduced an atmosphere of race-baiting into the election process that'd been somewhat absent from national politics in the previous few decades. The tactic was not new to American politics, of course, especially before the abolition of slavery, but it had always had the same nefarious goal—for politicians to gain control and feed upon the worst intentions and fears of Americans, winning votes based on fear rather than on issues and facts.

BY 1993, THOUGH Bill Clinton had been elected president, voters were beginning to become more enamored of these fear-based ideas, and began electing more conservative and then even more radically conservative members of the Republican Party to Congress. These new candidates and members of Congress waged an outright war on the poor, portraying them as welfare queens and criminals, all on the dole, who were too lazy to get a job. They were uninterested in hearing about the systematic injustices the families of South Central L.A. faced or even in acknowledging that African Americans were and are actually not even the greatest number of participants in the welfare system; white women are. So conservatives' hard-line interest in cutting out and cutting off support for the poor, and moving people from "welfare to work," as President Clinton would say, would actually hurt their constituents even more than the Black community.

They would have just as soon written off the L.A. Rebellion as the actions of thugs and criminals, and thrown them all into a soon-to-be-built private prison so that some of their rich friends could monetize their hardship for millions of dollars. It was a terribly challenging situation to be a Black woman in the House in 1993, but still, Waters looked for every opening. She was unafraid and unashamed to approach conservative members with new ideas that could resonate. She never accepted the marginalization and the disdain that society projected toward her constituents. She defended their humanity and fought for every single inch of dignity and respect.

Case in point, Rep. Charles Stenholm, who had been a member of Congress since 1979. He was an old-line Democrat from Texas, from the strain of Democrats who implemented Jim Crow segregation in the Deep South. But his politics were not based in identity, but more in fiscal discipline and Christian values. He was a traditional conservative, not a member of the radical breed that Newt Gingrich and others personified. He was a member of the Blue Dog Coalition, a group of conservative Democrats who believed that the Democratic Party was moving too far to the left and was not speaking to the fundamental needs of constituents like his. All his constituents wanted was a fair shot at making a decent living. They wanted a chance to make it in a world where they were, for the first time, being left out and left behind. They blamed this abandonment on the greater focus on a social agenda, but actually it was the conservative war against support for the middle class and the poor that was at fault. They had a way of life. They were the farmers of rural Texas. They loved the land. They didn't want to move to a big city; they wanted to have a fighting chance to live the way they had always lived for generations, but because so much had been given over to big agricultural interests, the average or even medium-sized farmer was working hard, but could not make ends meet.

Stenholm had been a staunch supporter of Ronald Reagan, and worked closely with the House Budget Committee chairman because he was concerned about the ever-increasing federal deficit. Reagan left the largest deficit in American history at the end of his presidency, a high-water mark later surpassed by George W. Bush. Clinton, the incoming president, a Democrat, would actually balance the budget. When he left office, the nation was "in the black" as they say in the world of finance. Stenholm, though a fan of Reagan, had opposed President George W. Bush's budget. He knew that the series of tax cuts Bush proposed would only add to the federal deficit. If any cataclysm happened—and of course it would, including the future war in Iraq and Hurricane Katrina, the nation would have fewer resources to help where it really counted. Stenholm thought cutting taxes at a time when the federal deficit was the largest it had ever been was irresponsible. Despite the fact that his district was becoming ever more red, he pushed back against the president's budget choices. Waters was looking for a partner to work with on an idea she had. She watched Stenholm closely. Even though they didn't agree on everything, she observed and liked his commitment to his principles. He stood for something. She liked that, so she made her approach.

In an interview in 1993 with *The Progressive*, Waters recalls,

> *Representative Stenholm had reduced the President's budget when it came to the House. I'm watching all this, and meanwhile, I'm watching Stenholm and I'm thinking, "I like his style. This guy gets things done." So I said to him, "Look, I want to talk to you about something. You want to cut the budget. I think we've got some serious problems out here. One that I'm very passionate about is all of these young minority males, Black and Latino for the most part, out on the street. They're wreaking havoc. You know what: I think if we say to them, "You've gotta do something with your life, you've got to enroll in school," we ought to be able to give them a little support. I think it's the best crime-prevention program in the world, the best birth-control program in the world, and I think that it just makes good sense. I'm not talking about a lot of money. I'm talking about 100 bucks a week for survival. We'll help you a little bit if you want to help yourself. I said, "This is self-help." And he bought it. He said, "You're right."*

Maxine Waters teamed up with Stenholm to maintain a job-training proposal, where millions of dollars would be allotted for job training for unemployed young people in both of their constituencies—whether Black or white; they'd also receive personal counseling and $100 per week in exchange for attending educational or vocational courses as well as apprenticeships. Waters designed the proposal with the youth of L.A. in mind. "I figured this would have appeal to the conservatives because I was talking about dealing with a group that could clearly be defined as a problem in America," she said. She had already put millions in an urban aid bill after the L.A. Rebellion. Under the Clinton administration she advocated for millions for summer jobs. Once again, Waters showed that she could work with people of all stripes.

★ ★ ★ ★ ★ ★ ★ ★ ★ ★ ★ ★ ★

RESISTANCE

If I want to fight,
I want to fight with
the lions.

—MAXINE WATERS, *THE WASHINGTON POST*

★

MAKING BANK

We got to fight the powers that be.
Fight the power.
—Public Enemy, "Fight the Power"

Maxine Waters joined the Financial Services Committee in 1991, and has served as either a ranking member or chair of almost all of the subcommittees under its jurisdiction since 1995. She joined Congress under House Majority Leader Rep. Richard Gephardt, and soon decided to learn as much as she could about how the money worked, hoping to find ways to increase investments in her district. She learned quickly that it was a committee dominated by white men. That was something that her presence could change ASAP. Yes, ma'am, white men were controlling the country's purse strings, and Maxine Waters was coming to cash in.

"Banking was of interest to me," Waters said in an interview with *Ebony* magazine in 1992, "because the committee deals with all the financial institutions that really determine the life and death of this country. . . . Whether we're talking about insurance or banking or mortgage interest, they [white men] control things. Even things that are strictly supported with tax dollars such as the Fed Home Loan Board, is headed by a White man with an all-White board of directors. They don't hire Blacks for any top positions. And we're talking about taxpayers' money! It's mindboggling and a real cause for anger. It's also cause for action to make sure that Blacks get their fair share. I intend to work on this for the next five years. I'm going to straighten some of these systems out!"

Assignment to such a committee is done through a system of seniority; members who have served longer get better positioning. At the time, it was called the House Committee on Banking and Currency, later changed to the Financial Services Committee, but whatever its name, it was the perfect committee for a Black woman with an agenda to lift her community out of poverty.

The Financial Services Committee is the House regulator of all the banks, credit card companies, savings and loans, stock and investment companies, real estate investment firms, securities firms, and insurance companies. It was smart thinking and good timing for a firm, pragmatic member like Auntie Maxine to join the committee, because the financial services industries, already quite powerful, would morph into trillion-dollar behemoths that would support and jeopardize American financial stability. But more on that in a second.

See, sis, a banking committee may not sound like a *lit* place to be, but Auntie Maxine's presence on the committee as a Black woman would be the best for the overall mission. She'd once again find herself where the need for inclusion was dire, and certain progressive actions had become stagnant. She'd be in the right place to give voice to the voiceless in one of the most powerful areas in our nation: money. Auntie Maxine's role and contribution on these committees would prove to be instrumental time and time again, in regulating but also in providing know-how of distributing and managing aid. It would be like going with your auntie to the mall; there were rules and a budget, but sometimes even more than your mama, she had your back. As two-time chairwoman of the Subcommittee on Housing and Community Opportunity, she authored the Neighborhood Stabilization Program and secured $6 billion in funding for grants to state and local governments and nonprofits to fight foreclosures and restore neighborhoods. In 2005, she was instrumental in advocating for the Bush administration to provide more aid to the community affected by Hurricane Katrina. Auntie Maxine had our back, and still does today—in fact, she's been accompanied by another Queen of the Resistance, Alexandria Ocasio-Cortez, who joined the committee in 2019. She also continues to look out for those communities of color abroad now as a leader spearheading efforts to try to cancel debt for vulnerable countries in Africa and Latin America.

See, to have a Black woman on this committee who had experienced poverty firsthand is the very definition of inclusion and intersectionality. Her job is to serve the nation, but her insight on Black lives is much, much needed in our nation, and before Auntie Maxine, one that was largely missing. A person of color at the top of their game like Maxine Waters would continuously reap fruit, and eventually in 2018, she'd become the first woman and first African American chair to lead the committee.

WATERS'S PREDECESSOR WAS Republican Jeb Hensarling of Texas, who decided to retire, and who served as an example of Waters's ability to work across the aisle on the committee. Together they attempted legislation like the JOBS Act 3.0—a package of thirty-two financial regulatory proposals including changes to credit access, investment disclosures, and capital-raising—but the bill did not leave the Senate.

However, one of her biggest areas of focus today and throughout her time on the committee has been a continuing battle royale, one that has been so brutal it could have been directed by Quentin Tarantino with an ending that would make Guillermo del Toro frightened: the battle with the Republican party to preserve the Consumer Financial Protection Bureau (CFPB), which was created by Queen of the Resistance Elizabeth Warren as a watchdog on consumer abuse and financial fraud.

Gurl, here's a refresher on the CFPB dating back to when Waters was a freshman member:

In her first years on the Banking Committee, Waters learned a lot, and eventually made a lot happen, just like she promised. From early on, her focus was on predatory lending, which had ripped and gutted the same communities of color that had been stomped, robbed, and taken advantage of throughout history. (This disrespect of POC is a running theme in this book, unfortunately, and yet some folks—assuming they are playing blind and deaf—still don't get how important doing better by these communities truly is to our nation's politics, so the authors shall persist!!!) Predatory lenders are banking institutions that take advantage of individuals living paycheck to paycheck. They may offer people with bad credit loans in advance of their paychecks at extremely high interest rates, with repayment deadlines that may be as little as two weeks, which sinks them deep into financial hardship. People can end up in a circumstance where lenders receive their paychecks, yet they *still* owe the creditors exorbitant rates of interest with no means to pay outside of getting another job. Dependence on payday loans can lead to bankruptcy. Payday lenders target poor people and often open up offices in poor neighborhoods. Through repeated measures, Waters has worked to rein in payday lenders. Currently, she is advancing bipartisan legislation to impose a strict limit on the interest payday lenders can charge. Payday lenders are barred by federal restrictions from offering veterans and active-duty military interest rates higher than 36 percent. Waters wants this cap imposed to protect all Americans.

Another key area where Waters contributed early on was to the Dodd–Frank Wall Street Reform and Consumer Protection Act, which came on the heels of the financial crisis of 2007, when the big banks began to engage in extremely risky financial practices.

In the 1950s and '60s, when banks granted mortgages, they generally held those mortgages until they were paid in full. But in the 1980s, banks lobbied to deregulate the mortgage-lending industry so that it became possible for banks to make mortgages, hold them for a time, and then sell them to another bank. Prime mortgages are mortgages made under optimum circumstances: the buyer has put down 20 percent, she has A1 credit ratings, a good salary and savings, no blemishes whatsoever. Subprime mortgages are mortgages made in conditions that are not optimal. That would mean: the borrower has had credit problems in the past, can only put down less than 20 percent, may not demonstrate a steady job history, or has just started a new job, has little savings, or the amount of the monthly payment represents more than one-third of the person's income, or the house is in a community that is less than desirable or could otherwise make it difficult to readily resell if the lender has to foreclose.

The crisis that began in the United States had economic repercussions worldwide. In the last six months of the Bush administration, Treasury Secretary Hank Paulson had advised the president and members of Congress that the banking industry was about to implode. Once again banks, this time the big banks, had been trading extremely risky kinds of subprime mortgages that destabilized not only the US market but the entire world financial market.

It used to be that mortgage lending was highly restricted to protect the stability of the largest investment most people will ever make in their lifetimes. But that had changed in recent years. What banks began to realize in the 2000s is that they made most of their profit on a loan at the beginning, that is why today many banks make a mortgage loan and sell it quickly to another party. They make the most interest possible on the money they lend, and then they can get the principal back through the sale and reinvest it right away, instead of making profit incrementally. They then further realized that, from a profit standpoint only, the *failure* of a mortgage works to their advantage, because they can charge high fees once the mortgage payments are slow in coming, then they can foreclose on the property and make a new mortgage where they will be making maximum profits again.

Eventually, banks began to see the subprime market as the

place where they could make the most money. Not only were subprime interest rates higher to begin with, when those mortgages failed, they could force borrowers in default to pay fees above the cost of interest on the mortgage, plus, somewhere out there, there would be yet another mortgage.

Banks began to target subprime borrowers, particularly African American and Latino homebuyers, and entice them to purchase homes or sign mortgage agreements that set them up to fail. They were being enticed by the opportunity to own the kind of home they had never been able to afford. Realtors and lenders made the homes sound affordable, touting low initial monthly payments, but buyers did not always fully understand the terms of these loans. They might, for example, after four years have to make a balloon payment or be tied to a variable interest rate that would change one's monthly payments whenever interest rates were raised.

These mortgages that were created to fail began to multiply inside the banking industry. They began to be so plentiful that banks created new financial instruments called credit default swaps in order to be able to trade them. The credit default swap allowed the investor to switch the risk they were engaging in by selling subprime mortgages to another investor, usually by making an ongoing payment that acted like an insurance policy. These instruments were almost like hot potatoes. They were fine as long as the borrower stayed afloat. But whoever owned the mortgage when the mortgage failed was the investor who had to manage the liability. Further, because these subprime mortgages began to be so plentiful and their quality was low, it became quite difficult to sell them.

Firms all across the industry had invested in the credit default swaps based on flimsy mortgages that were likely to fail, so Paulson knew there was a serious problem.

And as the failures actually began to happen, homeowners who had bought into the American dream and purchased houses were being evicted from their homes. There were 2.25 million mortgage foreclosures a year between 2010 and 2012, as well as millions more people whose homes were underwater, meaning their home's purchase price was now higher than the home's current value. Once the bottom dropped out of the housing market, people were stuck in overpriced houses with mortgages they couldn't afford, and they couldn't move or sell because they wouldn't be able to pay off their mortgages if they did sell.

Now, here's where the story gets a bit tricky. Paulson and some of his banker friends decided that the way to resolve the problem was not to simply allow banks to suffer the repercussions of their shoddy practices, which would actually have been the solution that true capitalism would determine. Instead of disciplining Wall Street, and allowing it to suffer the repercussions of its actions and climb its way out, as they did with the many millions of people who had believed the sweet talk of their mortgage brokers, Paulson decided the best solution was to reach into the US Treasury and basically give the big banks like Goldman Sachs, Chase, and Wells Fargo (one of the biggest offenders in the crisis) hundreds of millions of dollars in loans taken directly from the federal Treasury and given to the banks who had created the problem in the first place. This "bank bailout," as it was called, happened in the last six months of the Bush administration. Thus, all the policymakers who implemented these ideas were able to ride off into the sunset, leaving a huge economic mess in their wake for the next president, Barack Obama, to handle.

The Republican majority in the House and Senate held hearings and made statements that blamed the people for the crisis, saying that it had all happened simply because people had wanted to live in more house than they could afford, instead of holding bankers accountable for creating the mess. People, especially those who were not financially savvy, like the elderly, minorities, and immigrants, had been particularly vulnerable, because they would likely not understand complex mortgage terms. They were blamed for getting ensnared in complex financial wheeling and dealing, and many had their lives ruined, but Wall Street bankers were bailed out and let off the hook.

The Republicans lost the House in the election of 2008, largely due to their handling of the mortgage crisis, and the economy slid into the Great Recession. There was a lot of talk about recovery, but millions of people were still struggling.

Obama would come up with a strategy to help Americans, called the Hardest Hit Fund, which would give billions in federal dollars to those who had been hardest hit, but the Treasury Department did not put strict stipulations on the disbursement of funds and added a clause that allowed states to ultimately use the money for any purpose it saw fit. Republican governors and state legislatures, which controlled most of the states in the union, did not want to be required by the federal government to use the money in any specific way and many states received federal dollars that they did not fairly disburse to communities that were hardest hit, especially minority communities. Some did use the funds to aggressively assist those who had been forced out of their hones, but many states, like Georgia, did not. Hundreds of thousands of homes in cities across the country were simply abandoned. Whole communities were left like ghost towns for years until the economy of everyday Americans began to recover. African Americans lost 50 percent of their wealth during the crisis. No program of intervention was directed at them, and mainly that wealth has never been regained. Their housing losses helped pave the way for gentrification in cities like Washington, DC, and New York. Young buyers became wary of purchasing homes, scared by what they had witnessed or experienced during the housing crisis. Real estate developers benefited from the failures by buying up large numbers of homes in cities like Atlanta and then renting those homes to residents seeking housing.

Democrats had been trying to get financial reforms for years, but the Wall Street lobby is very powerful, and though there were many advocates for change, the banks always fought them. After the debacle of the mortgage crisis, banks were more willing to accept that restrictions would have to be imposed, which set the stage for a series of economic reforms that helped retard the return of this crisis.

It was up to the new administration, and the new Congress, to make a difference. And there Auntie Maxine stood. *Dun dun duunnn.* One of the first actions of the Obama administration had to be financial regulatory reforms. The House Financial Services Committee and the Senate Finance Committee, headed by Rep. Barney Frank (MA) and Sen. Chris Dodd (CT), led the process that culminated in the Dodd–Frank Wall Street Reform and Consumer Protection Act, the first major act to create significant, lasting reforms.

As a senior member of the House committee, Maxine Waters was heavily involved in work on the bill. Dodd–Frank made sweeping reforms that touched every federal agency that regulated Wall Street, reorganizing the regulatory system that has the power to oversee, inquire, investigate, and penalize the illegal actions of Wall Street. The bill consolidated federal financial regulatory agencies so that they could more completely and efficiently monitor the activity of Wall Street. It set up a new financial oversight body called the Financial Stability Oversight Council, as well as the Office of Financial Research, so that the federal government would have the capacity to identify threats to the financial markets before they became so massive the entire economy was affected. Elizabeth Warren, then a private citizen and professor at Harvard, consulted with the House and Senate as one of the top legal minds in the country with expertise in housing finance.

Unsurprisingly, Dodd–Frank, and Elizabeth Warren, were taking up a banner that our Auntie Maxine had long been flying. For years, she had been pushing for the establishment of a federal agency that could protect consumers from bad actions in the financial services industry. President Obama had also begun to support her proposals. Waters, along with others like future senator and queen Elizabeth Warren, ultimately convinced Sen. Dodd to include consumer protection in his package of reforms, and thus the Consumer Financial Protection Bureau (CFPB), an entirely new agency of government, was created. The bureau provided consumers with a government organization powerful enough to go after financial multinationals like the big banks when they felt like they were being defrauded by these powerful companies. The CFPB has jurisdiction over many of the financial businesses that touch consumer lives, like credit unions, stock brokerages, payday lenders, mortgage servicers, foreclosure relief services, student loans, and debt collectors. The bureau brings together the oversight responsibilities that had been dispersed throughout different parts of the government in agencies like the Federal Reserve, the Federal Trade Commission, and the Federal Deposit Insurance Corporation, to name a few, into one independent branch of government.

The CFPB can create and enforce rules and regulations that restrict freewheeling or predatory practices in financial services businesses. It can examine financial businesses, monitor and report on the health of financial markets without Wall Street influence, and collect consumer complaints and pursue claims against financial industries to protect the American people. Its purpose is to "make markets for consumer financial products work for Americans—whether they are applying for a mortgage, choosing credit cards . . . or using any number of other consumer financial products."

Whenever a financial institution acquires $10 billion in assets it falls under the jurisdiction of CFPB, which reviews and examines that institution's activities to ensure that it is following regulatory policies. Waters, as a senior member of the committee that wrote the Dodd–Frank legislation, was critically involved in the discussion and creation of the bill. Waters advocated for and won the creation of an Office of

Women and Minorities as a way to encourage more diversity in the financial services industry. *Hurrah.*

DODD–FRANK GAVE THE Federal Reserve new powers to oversee the liquidation of large companies. One reason the Bush administration gave for doling out millions of the people's money to for-profit institutions, is that some companies are "too big to fail." In other words, some organizations are pillars of the American financial system. They manage so many of the nation's assets and the resources of millions of people, if they were allowed to fail, even if the cause of that failure was due to mismanagement that it should otherwise be held accountable for, the impact of that failure would be so cataclysmic to the American financial system and economy as well as the world economy, that it is in the best interest of the nation to invest resources in the survival of that entity, rather than allow market forces to push it into bankruptcy.

The purpose of Dodd–Frank was to prevent this kind of cataclysmic impact in the financial markets from ever happening again. It is one of the key accomplishments of the Obama presidency. However, in the Trump era, the financial services companies have pushed back, especially while Republicans had control of the House, and tried to nullify or at least revise the regulatory authority provided in Dodd–Frank. Some analysts say the financial services industry is again

engaged in questionable practices that could lead to another debacle on Wall Street.

In 2017, Auntie Maxine called for the complete shutdown of Wells Fargo Bank after numerous scandals, such as the bank creating millions of fake accounts for unwitting consumers and charging people for car insurance they didn't need. They weren't shut down, but the CFPB hit them with a $1 billion fine. In 2017, Waters wrote a thirty-eight-page report, reminding everyone of Wells Fargo's practices back in 2007. In 2019 she told *Vox*: "It seems as if they can't get their act together." She also referenced Equifax, the credit-reporting firm, for compromising the data of 150 million people in 2017. Waters also produced the Comprehensive Credit Reporting Reform Act and the Megabank Accountability and Consequences Act.

The wonderful news is that even as chairwoman of the Financial Services Committee, Auntie Maxine still remains the unapologetic queen from St. Louis. She is not afraid to keep fighting back. At eighty-one years old, Maxine Waters is was still getting promoted, ladies, becoming the chair of the committee in 2018. The glass ceiling is just the start. Auntie Maxine is letting nothing stop her, by way of justice. She said it best to *Ebony* magazine: "Being a Black elected official in America, it's never easy. I choose to do this work. . . . I have never taken the easy way out because I don't think you get anything done that way."

From Project Build to Dodd–Frank, protecting the financial interests and economic improvement of American lives, especially looking out for African Americans via the Financial Services Committee, Auntie Maxine has the resilience, tenacity, and skill that, as always, makes her a true Queen of the Resistance.

DON'T CALL ME MAXINE

My name is not Susan
So watch what you say.
—Whitney Houston, "My Name Is Not Susan"

L et's backtrack to the queen's early years in Congress for a few important reminders.

As a freshman member of Congress in 1991, the same year that she joined the Financial Services Committee, Maxine Waters was also on the Veterans' Affairs Committee. No sooner had Waters arrived in Washington than she once again had a Goliath that she'd have to conquer. She joined the committee knowing that she was the only woman and only Black person. The committee chair was Sonny Montgomery from Mississippi, a retired National Guard member with a reputation for being strict. *Oh, sis, I know, how are these two going to mesh, right?* He was known for running the committee with an iron fist, *eek.*

Waters wasn't afraid. *Did we expect her to be?*

Montgomery was equally notorious for having no, zero, zilch tolerance for lateness. But Auntie Maxine had trouble finding the room that first day. It was on a different floor from what she expected, and in the end, she arrived a few minutes late. She walked in and sat down quietly, took a look around the room—white man, white man, white man, and so on. It was all white men, as they'd said. Auntie Maxine is no punk at all, and what she told Angela Rye on *On the One* is that she thought: *Huh, he better not mess with me.* (Auntie is gangsta, y'all!)

Montgomery, a former state trooper, was not one to be messed with either. Black, white, woman, man . . . What these two did have in common was a notorious bite-back.

Anyway, the conversation starts rolling around the room. Everyone sharing their two cents. As the newbie, Waters wanted to put in her opinion about costs. She was perplexed about the prevailing notion that Montgomery didn't seem to want any of the committee members to propose anything that cost money, which she found ridiculous. If the funding for a bill got turned down, that was fine, but to not even ask? . . . Well, that wasn't at all what Auntie Maxine had learned legislation is all about. When it was her turn to speak, she said this to him in her own way, which is usually straightforward, and of course he didn't like it.

He disagreed, of course, but when he decided to be vindictive and salty about it and pop off in front of everyone about Auntie having been only a few minutes late on her first day, *Oh Lord, help him. . . .*

"By the way, *Maxine*, this committee starts on time."

Maxine, huh? . . . Maxine, who?

Auntie probably started to see stars fire—WTH was he saying? Maxine? Did he know her from family picnics, did they go to the salon together, was he in her swim class? No. Then why the heck was he calling her by her first name? No, no, no, sir. She was a freshman in an all-male locker room, a fifty-three-year-old woman, and there was no need to hesitate or try to win friends anyway, but she caught herself. She bit her tongue. She told Angela Rye that she took a deep breath to let it sit for a while. *Breathe. Breathe. Breathe.* She asked herself therapeutic questions: *Was it a problem that he called her Maxine? Did he mean anything by calling her by her first name?* Hmmm. *Was he calling her Maxine like the* help, *"Hey, maid Maxine, come to work on time"?* Hmmm. *Was she not a member of Congress?* she remembered thinking. She collected Aunt Jemima figurines due to her respect for their history, but there was no way that she'd be treated like an underling today. (To Auntie Maxine, Aunt Jemima memorabilia represented the endurance of Black women who came before her. "They have so much wisdom. They worked hard, they scrubbed floors, they raised the children, they nurtured their men. I just love that this Black woman, as exemplified by Aunt Jemima, is probably what held this race together.")

The problem of the moment was really his audacity to even go there. Had he ever or would he ever think to address a male member this way? It was pure shade. Hell no, she wasn't going to allow that, but she bit her lip the entire meeting. She explained to Rye when to throw shade and when to hold back:

I have this thing about life. You fit your lines of action. If I am at a cocktail party, talking nicey-nice, if I'm in a back room where the fight is on, I know how to say son-of-a-bitch as well as anybody, and will fight as hard as anybody. But it really is [about] fitting your lines of action. I don't pretend to be happy all the time. I don't pretend to be nice no matter what. I don't take insults no matter what. Some people are trained to do that better than others. When you've basically come from a poor background, you're not really trained that way. I didn't go to finishing school.

But right after the meeting, when first-name-calling Montgomery was packing up all his notes and was ready to shuffle back down the hall to his office with all of his bros, Auntie Maxine waited to the side until there was room for her to move in on him calm and smoothly, and when she did, she said, as she told Rye, "I need to see you." He was thrown. She continued, "Don't you ever, first of all, call me by my first name. You don't know me. Usually around here, people are referred to as the gentleman or the gentlelady, Mr. This, or That or the Other." And she explained that's the way he should refer to her from now on.

Many times these sort of bad first encounters, when two *bosses* come head to head, can engender a mutual respect, and in this case with Waters and Montgomery, even a friendship. She wasn't afraid to tell him the truth about his committee from her perspective as a woman and person of color. She made it known quickly that he needed to make certain changes. Gurl, Auntie Maxine came down on him like your mama when she discovers the mess you've been hiding in your room and she pays the rent; to her, his blind spots were ridiculous. One great thing about Auntie is that she goes into these situations and she's able to see them for what they are. She didn't go into his committee as the only Black woman ready to bend and fold according to his will and standards like she'd landed there because she held some lucky lottery ticket. No. She worked her butt off to get in the room. Instead, he would bend and fold to her. At the next meeting (*no, she did not wait longer, what are you thinking?! This is Auntie Maxine*) she told him that she found it *really* freakin' strange, actually baffling, that he was chairing a committee for veterans and there was not a Black person in the room till she got there.

After all, there are millions of Black men and women sacrificing their lives and time with their families in these wars, the Persian Gulf, Vietnam . . . Where are the brothas and

sistas, bruh? Black people are veterans too. There were fifty-five staff positions and she was the first Black person?

Auntie Maxine called it out on day two, sister. You don't need to wait.

Of course, there was more stuttering, she said. "He made some excuses. He told me that he had one minority on the staff one time and he drowned; he died. Then he told me that he had tried to get one to come up from Mississippi and he didn't want to come there. I said there are plenty of African Americans here in Washington, DC." *OH. MY. GOD.* He couldn't find someone alive and Black in DC? These are the "excuses" about the lack of diversity in most American corporate offices, committees, boards, and so on that Auntie Maxine does not have any time for—she does not accept it—and we shouldn't accept it either.

Waters wasn't there to fight. She was there to make change. Someone had to say it to this man, but no one had been at the table to do it. Here she was. Ready for it.

So, in the end, he basically went out and found some Black people (*yes, they were right there, after all!*), and the committee became more diverse than ever. All thanks to Auntie Maxine, of course.

IN HER NEW post, Rep. Waters came out of the shadows with the L.A. Rebellion, and got the attention of her colleagues, but the tipping point as to when Congress really began to under-stand the force that was on their hands with Maxine Waters on staff was at the Banking Committee's Whitewater hearings in 1994.

Rep. Peter King of Long Island must have suddenly forgot who he was and thought that he was King Kong when he was questioning former Hillary Clinton staffer Margaret Williams. It got so aggressive that the chair accused King of badgering Williams. Like a feminist *boss*, Maxine Waters jumped to Williams's defense as well.

But then King made a fatal error. He said to Auntie Maxine, "You had your chance. Why don't you just sit there?"

Who? Did he really say that to Maxine Waters?

"You are out of order," she warned.

"You are always out of order," he spat back, like a six-year-old with a bad attitude.

"You are out of order," she repeated. "Shut up."

But then he tried to get into the ring with Auntie Maxine again by bringing it up the next day. *Did he not get the warning?* He brought it all on himself, as they say.

Auntie Maxine was not scheduled to speak that day, but she unapologetically strode right up to the mic, interrupting the hearing. Waters said, "Men and women, the day is over when men can badger and intimidate women!"

Rep. Carrie Meek of Florida started pounding away at the

gavel, but Waters continued. Representatives were yelling all over the place, many shouting in King's defense. Someone called out for the mace. *What's the mace?* Half the room of political junkies and intellectuals looked around, confused; they didn't know what a mace was. But something needed to stop this Maxine Waters. There was an angry Black woman on the loose, run! Someone, *pleeaase*, get the book about maces. No, it was not the pepper spray, though King's behavior called for that. Finally, amid all the fracas, they found that a mace was a ceremonial staff used to remove members who need to be quieted.

But the room was in an oily flux; Rep. Meek struggled with deciding on using the mace and instead just kept slamming her gavel down, as Maxine Waters would not relent. (See, Auntie Maxine is not afraid of the "Black woman" label; it doesn't scare her. She refuses to let it quiet her. Look at all the beautiful women who have gotten the label and still rise: Serena Williams, Michelle Obama, Jemele Hill, Melissa Harris-Perry—all exceptional women.) Maxine Waters would not be quieted. "We are members in this House. We will not allow men to intimidate us and to keep us from participating."

"You must suspend! You must suspend, gentlewoman!" demanded Rep. Meek.

But she didn't. Rep. Meek could not get the crowd under

control no matter how many times she tried. The more Maxine Waters went on, the more members heckled her.

And the chaos did not end until Auntie Maxine said so, when she walked right out of the room.

The Republican representatives wanted her disciplined for interrupting a hearing and disturbing *their* peace. It was a witch hunt, and they wanted Maxine Waters burned at the stake. In an interview with *Los Angeles* magazine in 1998, she addressed the event: "I think that my strong position and my advocacy are what my constituents really want and like. I make things happen, and I have credibility with the people I care about . . . I have the ability to listen even if I am going to disagree. And I disagree a lot. But I can do it in a way that does not necessarily disrespect them. But they have also learned that I cannot be run over. I cannot be abused. I cannot be disrespected."

She was never disciplined like they wanted, and while Clinton was impeached, it wasn't directly connected to Whitewater. But in regard to their question about the new member, *Who does this Maxine Waters think she is?* Bwa-ha-ha-ha.

THE CONSCIENCE OF THE CONGRESS

I never knew a luh, luh-luh, a love like this.
—Common, "The Light"

I n 1996, Auntie Maxine was elected to chair the Congressional Black Caucus (CBC). In the 1960s, more African Americans were entering the House of Representatives, and they wanted to have a joint representation of their own. The CBC was founded in 1969. Originally they were the Democratic Select Committee but were renamed the Congressional Black Caucus in 1971. They would also be nicknamed the "Conscience of the Congress." There were thirteen founding members, twelve of them men. The sole woman was Shirley Chisholm. Charles Diggs, the first African American to represent Michigan, and a civil rights activist, was the first chairperson. Diggs was largely known as being the only member of Congress to attend the Emmett Till murder trial back in 1955, where he was forced to sit in the back of the room with the one other Black journalist.

This was the sort of precedent that a chair of the CBC is based on—fearlessness, action, and a love for justice that moves one to places even where he or she is unwelcome. In 1971, Diggs and the other founding members forced their presence to be taken seriously when they boycotted President Nixon's State of the Union Address after he refused to meet with them.

The CBC may have started with thirteen members, but today those numbers have tripled as they help new Black lawmakers. Maxine Waters was the third woman to be elected chair of the organization. The first was Rep. Yvonne Brathwaite Burke in 1976 and the second was Rep. Cardiss Collins. Waters was nominated by Rep. Eva Clayton, the first African American to represent North Carolina. Yes, once again a woman helping to push Auntie forward! By this time, since the lone Chisholm star, there were now twelve women members of the CBC and under Rep. Waters's leadership.

In 1996, being the chair of the CBC was not an easy task. The House was controlled by the Republicans, and Auntie Maxine had the double challenge of being one of the few women they'd seen in that seat for twenty-six years, and being a Democrat. The benefit was that she was Maxine Waters, and anyone who cometh up against the queen would need to provide answers when addressed. In fact, some of her colleagues were even worried about this, but most were in agreement that the muscle of Maxine was exactly what the

CBC needed. It was a role that she considers to be one of her great accomplishments. She told *Black Enterprise*, "The Congressional Black Caucus is very effective. Much of the work that we do is stopping bad things from happening. All of the work of the caucus is not seen simply in producing a piece of paper. Yes, we're working in a hostile environment with Republicans in charge. [They] don't agree with the Black agenda, and that's why we work so hard to get them out of office. To the degree that Republicans are not in charge, we're more successful. When the Republicans are in charge, certainly we have to work harder."

Waters and the CBC also spent the 1990s investigating the controversy over whether the US intelligence agencies contributed to the crack epidemic in Los Angeles. Crack came on the scene in the 1980s. It was a drug produced by crystallizing cocaine into a smokeable powder substance that was cheaper to make, less expensive than cocaine, and had an immediate euphoric effect that made it addictive. It was easy to produce and sell, so the demand grew rapidly, and it was killing the Black community just as fast. It could be sold for $5–20 per vial. Between 1982 and 1985, 1.6 million people were crack cocaine users. The name came from the crackling sound it makes when smoked. Due to how cheap it was to make and that it brought in large profits, it was known as a poor man's drug. The poor or low-income communities like South Central, Watts, and other inner-city areas around the country were drastically affected. Crack led to more and more independent drug dealers, more than one on every corner, as well as drug wars, Black men and women losing their jobs and homes, users succumbing to a zombielike state, and Black families being ripped apart.

The crime rate skyrocketed. The Reagan administration created the War on Drugs program to stop drug trafficking, but to keep it *100*, it was really a war on young, Black males. Their efforts included passing federal anti-drug laws and increasing antidrug funding, which would have been fine if it hadn't resulted in 1 in every 4 Black men between the ages of twenty and twenty-nine being under the supervision of the criminal justice system. By 1995, when Maxine Waters and other lawmakers in the CBC were still looking for answers, that number was 1 in 3. The War on Drugs included the expansion of police and prison programs, legislation, and cruel penalties for the targeted, including incredibly harsh mandatory minimum sentences. The focus wasn't on resources to get the drug users help, but to remove them from the streets by any means. For possessing just five grams of crack cocaine, a minimum of five years was given to both users and dealers. The prisons were jam-packed with Black bodies. So when there were allegations or claims that the US government was involved, Waters was all over it, honey. It's still a controversial issue, and the connections to the Iran–Contra Affair remain unanswered. But the odds are good that Auntie Maxine is still pounding the pavement, and getting answers, today.

THE HIV/AIDS EPIDEMIC would directly coincide with the crack epidemic. It was hitting areas that were high in poverty. The poor, who didn't have the resources to educate their communities about the disease, often didn't have Medicaid, either. In the early '80s, HIV was labeled as a disease for gay white men, but Maxine Waters led the charge to show how minority communities were under a "state of emergency" due to the many outbreaks there. From 1986 to 1998 new AIDS cases had increased from 25 to 45 percent among African Americans and 14 to 22 percent new cases among Latinos. Similar to the crack epidemic, the disease had become one of the leading killers of Black men, especially those ages twenty-five to forty-four.

Waters testified before the Appropriations Subcommittee of Labor, HHS, and Education, "The Congressional Black Caucus has prioritized education targeting this group. There is a desperate need to communicate the dangers of drugs in an accessible, contemporary way that reaches young people in particular, in at-risk populations. This needs to be done in a way that explains in a precise, detailed, and stark manner the risks and damage that come with drugs including death, incarceration, AIDS, and other terrible consequences."

In 1999 Waters, along with the Congressional Black Caucus and the Clinton administration, spearheaded the initial appropriation, which was $156 million. With it, she helped to create funding to treat the spread of HIV in minority communities. She has also been a strong advocate for HIV/AIDS awareness. She's introduced legislation to address the HIV/AIDS epidemic in the African American community since she was an assemblywoman. Now as a member of Congress, she would help to establish the Minority AIDS Initiative to expand prevention campaigns, screening, and treatment efforts in minority groups. It would place more addicts in drug treatment and patients in medical care. Compare with Reagan's War on Drugs—this initiative was taking care to help the Black community, not shut it down. Waters also worked to eliminate mandatory minimum sentences for offenses related to crack cocaine under the Controlled Substances Act and the Controlled Substances Import and Export Act. (If a better tolerance had been brought to bear during the crack epidemic, more young Black men would have been home with their families instead of being held in jail.)

Auntie Maxine was always looking out for her constituents, but it went much deeper than that. She also had to protect them.

FROM CUBA WITH LOVE

My emancipation don't fit your equation.
—Lauryn Hill, "Lost Ones"

On the night of May 2, 1973, on the southbound side of the New Jersey Turnpike, a Black woman and two Black men were stopped for a motor vehicle violation. Soon, they got into a tussle with two white state troopers. The woman, Joanne Chesimard, more widely known as Assata Shakur, a Black Panther known as the "mother hen" of the Black Liberation Army, was wanted for several alleged felonies, including bank robbery. She was in the car with her best friend, Zayd Shakur, and the driver and fellow Panther Sundiata Acoli. Another theme of this book is the liberties police take with Black people, and sadly, the cause for the stop was foggy, but the scene turned heated quickly, and shots were fired. Sundiata fled across the highway, where he got away. Zayd was shot and killed. One of the troopers, Werner Foerster, was shot twice in the head and killed with his own rifle. Assata tried to flee but was caught. She raised her hands in air, according to three medical experts, but was still shot three times. She was hospitalized. Sundiata was later captured and jailed. Assata was beaten and psychologically tortured in the hospital, where she was held for pretrial. The other trooper, James Harper, testified at her trial, and in 1977, Assata Shakur was found guilty of first-degree murder, assault and battery of a police officer, assault with a dangerous weapon, assault with intent to kill, illegal possession of a weapon, and armed robbery—all by an all-white jury. She was sentenced to life in prison and taken to the Clinton Women's Prison in New Jersey.

The Black Panther Party was an organization that was focused on creating housing, education, and food for African Americans in the late 1960s. Malcolm X was gone. Martin Luther King had been assassinated on a hotel patio. Known for their leather jackets and long round afros, Panthers resisted police brutality and carried guns for self-defense. FBI director J. Edgar Hoover called them the "greatest threat to the security of the United States." He created COINTELPRO, a secret organization to "neutralize" them. As the Black community understood it, Assata Shakur was part of that "neutralization."

On November 2, 1979, the Black Liberation Army and Black Panthers helped Assata Shakur escape from prison. In the years that followed, she lived underground before eventually fleeing to Cuba. In all those years, hardly anyone knew her whereabouts. Apparently she was writing, had gotten married, and had more children. She'd given birth to a daughter already, while on trial for murder.

Then in 1998, she was spotted. The US government was informed, and the hunt for her began.

Enter Auntie Maxine.

The US government was still pouting about Assata Shakur and her great escape. But Black people still revered her as a leader of the Black Panther Party. In 1998, New Jersey governor Christine Todd Whitman reordered the extradition of Shakur, and the New Jersey State Police issued a $100,000 reward.

But the FBI did a sneaky thing when requesting the extradition. Auntie Maxine and the Congressional Black Caucus signed off on the request because the FBI had used Shakur's birth name, Joanne Chesimard, and her alias Assata Shakur was not mentioned anywhere in the documents. The US House of Representatives enacted HR 254, calling for her immediate extradition, but once Maxine Waters caught on that it was actually Assata Shakur, she swiftly called shenanigans and rescinded her position. "Assata Shakur was a member of the Black Panther Party, the [FBI's] primary target of . . . persecution . . . [This] was wrong in 1973, and remains wrong today." She wrote a letter directly to Fidel Castro right away, explaining what happened. After mistakenly voting for a House resolution for Cuba to extradite Shakur, Waters called out the trickery of Republican officials for not referring to her as Assata Shakur. And when Auntie sits down to write a letter, oh gurl, we know things happen.

LETTER TO FIDEL

I support the right of all nations to grant political asylum to individuals fleeing political persecution. . . . [I]t is the inviolate right of legitimate governments to grant asylum pursuant to the principles of the Universal Declaration of Human Rights. . . . Just as we maintain the right to grant political asylum for individuals from Cuba, we must respect the right of the government of Cuba to grant political asylum for individuals from the U.S. fleeing political persecution. . . . The second reason I oppose this measure is because I respect the right of Assata Shakur to seek political asylum. Assata Shakur has maintained that she was persecuted as a result of her political beliefs and political affiliations. As a result, she left the United States and sought political asylum in Cuba, where she still resides. In a sad and shameful chapter of our history, during the 1960s and 1970s, many civil rights, Black Power and other politically active groups were secretly targeted by the FBI for prosecution based on their political beliefs. . . . [T]he most vicious and reprehensible acts were taken against the leaders and organizations associated with the Black Power or Black Liberation Movement. Assata Shakur was a member of the Black Panther Party, one of the leading groups associated with the Black Liberation Movement.

THAT WOULDN'T BE the only time Auntie Maxine stepped in internationally—in fact, she remains just as dedicated to foreign affairs and the Black lives across the world as she is to those at home. Her loyalty to the Haitian people both here and in Haiti has been immense and ongoing.

In 2004, it started with a phone call. Her home phone rang at six A.M. Auntie Maxine answered. It was Mildred Trouillot, the wife of Haitian president Jean-Bertrand Aristide. "The coup d'état has been completed," is all that the First Lady said before passing the phone to her husband. According to CNN, a frightened President Aristide went on to tell Waters that the chief of staff of the US embassy had come to their home and said that he [Aristide] would be killed and "a lot of Haitians would be killed." He said that he followed their orders, and that he, his wife, his brother, and two security members were taken to the airport and were forced to leave.

Aristide, a former Roman Catholic priest, was Haiti's first democratically elected president in 1991, but was ousted in a military coup just seven days into his term. The coup collapsed in a US military invasion three years later. He was restored to the presidency from 1994 to 1998 and reelected in

2000. He claimed to have been ousted due to the ex-army paramilitary groups that invaded Haiti from across the border with the Dominican Republic where they were gathered and were creating havoc in the northern part of the country— killing civilians and Fanmi Lavalas, the political party associated with Aristide. He told officials that the US government had helped participate in his abduction.

Waters and Rep. Charles Rangel of New York were among those Aristide trusted to confide in, and they went public with their information. They had been faithful aides to Haiti in the past. Back in 1994, Waters had already visited many times, and Aristide was well respected in the Congressional Black Caucus. When the news got back to Congress, Bush denied it, Secretary of State Colin Powell said the accusation was baseless—basically, they called Aristide a liar. Powell told a different story. He said that Aristide left the country with fifteen security members, his own detail. He said that there was no way Aristide was forced out; in fact, Aristide had called the US ambassador to Haiti, James Foley, the night before to ask for advice and concluded himself that resigning would be the best course of action. He wanted to talk to his wife about it. His security detail was in alignment and they left the country of their own will. Aristide wrote a resignation letter, a leased plane was brought in, and he departed.

It was a confusing story for the media, but Auntie Maxine thought about how this would affect the Haitian people in

America and their families abroad. The media was reporting that Haitians were so desperate to get away from the political unrest that many were trying to flee to the United States to escape it. She owed it to them to help. "The way I see it is that they came to his house uninvited. They had not only the force of the embassy but the marines with them. They made it clear that they had to go now or he would be killed. It was very clear to him that the Americans had been responsible for carrying out a coup d'état . . . I have a lot of questions of my own government at this point. President Aristide said it was a coup."

Auntie Maxine had dedicated over twenty-five years to American politics, and she'd been lied to before and therefore she wanted to get the record of accounts straight. By March, Auntie Maxine had worked it out with Bush whereby she and the founder of TransAfrica, Randall Robinson, and a few others, including Aristide's lawyer, could accompany Aristide and his wife to Jamaica, where he had been invited by the prime minister to stay for a long visit. (He would remain in exile for seven years, returning to Haiti in 2011.)

Waters continues to defend the rights of political prisoners in Haiti. She has continued to support elections in Haiti and has been a voice in the United States to lean for UN backing. And in response to the January 2010 earthquake, she helped to secure debt relief for Haiti from financial institutions such as the World Bank and International Monetary Fund. Once Auntie Maxine invests her love, it's constant.

★

PEACE NOT WAR

*They got money for wars
but can't feed the poor.*
—Tupac, "Keep Ya Head Up"

oney, Maxine Waters had *a lot* of other problems with the Bush administration. Starting with the strange way he got into office. In the 2000 presidential election, George W. Bush was in a race against incumbent vice president Al Gore. The race was close. As voters began to nod off into dreamland after staying up late to watch what was one of the tightest, and most stressful, races in the nation's history to date, it was unclear who'd won in Florida. At eight P.M., it looked as if Gore had won, a few hours later, Bush. Finally after a recount, which Gore requested be hand-counted, the results showed that Bush won by 537 votes. Dang. Similar to our current president's election, there were some faulty and shady processes going on. *side-eye* (See a pattern here?)

That year, Maxine Waters was named chair of the Democratic Caucus Special Committee on Election Reform. She became laser-focused on putting a stop to faulty elections and to ensure that voters' rights were no longer infringed upon. They met with disenfranchised voters. They held hearings with voters in Florida but also around the country, in Los Angeles, Chicago, Philadelphia, and San Antonio. They created a report that recommended minimum national standards in handling of provisional ballots, purging of voter lists, accessibility for seniors and persons with disabilities and the visually impaired, non-English speakers, and Election Day voter registration databases. They were on a mission to pass meaningful legislation to reform the system. By 2001, she, along with other members of Congress created the Voting Rights Institute of the Democratic National Committee. It was established to monitor developments in election law and to advocate for making voting more accessible, as well as to provide guidance on voting rights and election administration issues.

And one of her biggest moments in opposition of Bush was when Maxine Waters voted against the Iraq War resolution, which was to fund the military action against the regime of Saddam Hussein. She supported the immediate withdrawal of troops and asserted that funds being used for the military occupation were draining American dollars. The funds that Bush continued to request could be used for resources that would improve the lives of Americans. Auntie Maxine continuously challenged the government's rhetoric about the Iraq

War. She became part of the House resolution to impeach Vice President Dick Cheney regarding false allegations about the war, the claims that he had undercut the CIA by asking that all intelligence be sent directly to him, and establishing an alternative agency in the Pentagon, along with Secretary of Defense Donald Rumsfeld.

Finally, after the March 2003 invasion of Iraq, the Pentagon's Defense Intelligence Agency concluded that "there is no reliable information on whether Iraq is producing and stockpiling chemical weapons, or where Iraq has—or will—establish its chemical warfare agent production facilities." The vice president had misrepresented this information in March 2002 when he said, "We know they have biological and chemical weapons" and later that year in August, "There is no doubt that Saddam Hussein now has weapons of mass destruction. There is no doubt that he is amassing them to use against our friends, against allies, and against us." Also despite a lack of evidence, he persisted in stating that there was a link between Iraq and Al Qaeda. Eventually Bush would acknowledge that he was involved in initiating harsh treatment of detainees during interrogations where they were blindfolded, strapped to a board, and held down while large amounts of water were poured into their faces.

By 2009, Auntie Maxine said in a floor statement, "The president would lead us to believe that there are only two options in Iraq; Congress must either continue to fund the war indefinitely, or we must choose to pull the rug out from under the troops and strand them in the field without body armor and bullets. This, of course, is a ridiculous characterization of our position. We feel that continuing to referee a civil war in Iraq runs counter to our national security interests. There is no military solution to the war in Iraq no matter how many soldiers, weapons, and dollars you dump into the country. Bombs and bullets have not and will not bring us peace in Iraq." It took almost a decade of persistent resistance by this queen of truth telling, but finally in 2011 the last convoy of US soldiers were pulled out of Iraq. It took nine years and thousands of American lives, and even more Iraqi lives.

★ ★ ★ ★ ★ ★ ★ ★ ★ ★ ★ ★ ★

QUEEN

You cannot be
successful and
continue to be
a victim.

—MAXINE WATERS, EXCERPTED FROM
IF CUBICLES COULD TALK BY KIM BEAMON

---★---

OUR AUNTIE, WITH LOVE

Our potential is unlimited.
We rise.
—Alicia Keys

This story ends with the beginning.

The day after the inauguration of Donald Trump on January 21, 2017, was the Women's March on Washington, the largest single-day protest in US history. Women were angry, sad, and ready to fight back. Women of color led the resistance. Tamika Mallory, executive director of the National Action Network; Carmen Perez, executive director of the Gathering for Justice; and Linda Sarsour, executive director of the Arab Association of New York, served as national co-chairs, along with Bob Bland. Planned Parenthood partnered with the march by providing staff. Other organizations that helped included the NAACP, AFL-CIO, MoveOn.org, Mothers of the Movement, Human Rights Watch, Black Girls Rock!, Emily's List, and many more. Over a million people traveled on the Washington Metro that day.

The march started on Independence Avenue, at the south-west corner of the Capitol Building, and ran down toward the National Mall. Many other marches took place worldwide, and the main march in Washington was streamed on social media platforms like Facebook, Twitter, and YouTube. In the United States, the number of marches was 408, and 673 worldwide. There were marches in Belgium, Kenya, Mexico, Costa Rica, Tanzania, and many more countries. There was even a march in Antarctica. Some 470,000 people came out to Washington. Five million people showed up in marches throughout the United States and 7 million worldwide.

It was a glorious day for Auntie Maxine, a feminist who had been fighting toward intersectionality and continuously pushing for the voices of Black woman to be heard. In the book *Together We Rise*, she described her experience at the march:

I had really begun to think that the women's movement was lost, that younger women didn't appreciate what we had done, and why. I thought they were more focused on their careers, thinking that a women's movement didn't enhance their opportunity for upward mobility, that they didn't want to be aligned with it. They didn't think they needed it . . . I lined up to speak, and I could not believe what I saw. I had heard there would be 250,000 people present; it was more like a million. It was unlike any

march I'd been to before . . . Going in, I had been feeling
disappointed, even a bit resentful, toward the younger gen-
eration. I was under the impression that they thought what
we had done for women's rights wasn't important. But see-
ing the size and passion of the crowd and realizing that the
younger women there recognized what we had done and
that they were carrying our torch made me realize I'd been
completely wrong . . . We walked from the stage all the
way to the White House and I was in a state of euphoria.

The march was a mecca of resistance. The Pussyhat Project pushed for the creation of pink hats that resembled female
genitalia, and people all around the country started crafting
the hats. There was a website for how to do it—whether sew-
ing, knitting, or crocheting, sis. Powerful women spoke at
the march, including America Ferrera, Gloria Steinem, Scar-
lett Johansson, Cecile Richards, Angela Davis, Ashley Judd,
Melissa Harris-Perry, Kamala Harris, Janet Mock, Janelle
Monáe, Kristin-Rowe Finkbeiner, Ai-jen Poo, Donna Hylton,
and many more amazing women. Alicia Keys performed,
okay.

The women were outraged by the president-elect. Auntie
Maxine was completely transparent about her feelings about
him from the very beginning, and so when he was elected,
she said publicly, "I've never seen anybody as disgusting or as
disrespectful as he is." She refused to go to Trump's inaugu-

ration. She didn't attend his first speech before Congress. She posted memes of Trump's administration as the Kremlin Klan, and said, "I don't honor this president. I don't respect this president. And I'm not joyful in the presence of this president." Damn, what a read, but that's exactly what many Americans felt. Auntie Maxine served the *tea* and the crackers, and she's called for his impeachment since his election.

Her resistance is based as much in policy as it is in calling out BS like the Tea Party. She said straight-up that "the Tea Party can go straight to hell." If you're trying to rummage through the mess of the Trump administration to find some clarification, Auntie Maxine will pave the way. She pushed for an investigation into Russian interference in the 2016 elections and Trump's possible collusion. In an interview with Refinery29, she said, "We are going to call Donald Trump to task. We're going to investigate. And we're going to use the power that we now have to make sure that the American people understand how dangerous this president is."

Auntie Maxine speaks the truth and has inspired others today to do the same. Other women in Congress are following her lead.

She has paved the way for new generations like Queens of the Resistance Alexandria Ocasio-Cortez, Ayanna Pressley, and Rashida Tlaib, who all serve on her committees. She has inspired and mentored women like Kamala Harris, and stood beside other strong women like Queens of the Resistance

Nancy Pelosi and Elizabeth Warren, ride-or-die style, through thick and thin for justice.

Auntie Maxine continues to embrace her nickname because she understands her legacy. We see you, Auntie! And she wants us to know that she sees us too. She wants us to know, "Young Black women are understanding that they, too, can not only be elected to office, they can lead this country. And I'm very pleased, so I don't want anybody to be discouraged, I don't want anybody to think, *I can't do that*. You can. You can do whatever you want to do. I want you to have the confidence and the understanding that you deserve success and you deserve to lead. I can't be here forever! You've got to come do this stuff, okay?"

ACKNOWLEDGMENTS

Our agent, Johanna Castillo, at Writers House, is a true Queen of the Resistance and must go at the top of our acknowledgments. Wow, she is the very definition of love, creativity, and strength. We absolutely would not have had this opportunity without her strong vision and ability to keep us in check to get it done. We adore and honor you, queen. You are a changemaker who made our lifelong dreams of being published authors come true. Anytime you call us to have tea in your kitchen, we'll be there ASAP.

Thank you to the wonderful team at Plume, who believed in this four-book series to celebrate these Queens of the Resistance. Special acknowledgments, high-fives, dabs, and e-hugs to our brilliant, kind, and badass queen editors, Jill Schwartzman and Marya Pasciuto, and to the Plume team, who kept up the strong sisterhood and encouragement through and through to get this project done! *Yes, we can!* Thank you to the queens: Amanda Walker, Jamie Knapp, Becky Odell, Katie Taylor, Caroline Payne, Leila Siddiqui, Tiffany Estreicher, Alice Dalrymple, LeeAnn Pemberton, Susan Schwartz, Dora Mak, and Kaitlin Kall—and two good-guy allies who need a special shout-out: the editor-in-chief, John Parsley, and the creative director, Christopher Lin. To our publisher, Christine Ball, a strong woman and leader from the moment we met her, we especially love the army you've built and the work that you continue to innovate. Thank you!

THANK YOU, THANK YOU, THANK YOU to our beloved Ava Williams, our research assistant. You didn't know what you were getting yourself into, lol, but your positive vibes and hard work held it up the entire time from beginning to end. Thank you for your warm and patient spirit throughout the process.

THANK YOU, THANK YOU, THANK YOU to the talented Jonell Joshua for your beautiful images and being a creative who could make it through all the deadlines with precision. You're the best, girlfriend!

Krishan would like to give a big shout-out to her personal sister circle, the women in her life who took the lead in helping with Bleu on those daylong playdates: my sister, Dominique Marie Bell, Raven Brown-Walters, Renee Brown-Walters, Lenica Gomez, Zaira Vasco. Special thanks to my crew at WeInspire—JLove, Brea Baker, and Taylor Shaw—and also to my mentors who guide me, especially Adrienne Ingrum, who has been a wonderful fountain of knowledge and inspiration throughout my path. This is for my mom, a Queen of the Resistance from Brooklyn and the Bronx, New York, who left us too soon but whom I felt watching over me from heaven smiling; and her twin, my loving auntie Amina Samad, who always came over with love and hugs to help throughout the process—I love and cherish you both so very much. Thank you to my son, Xavier Bleu Jeune, for being such an awesome growing boy. I love being #BleusMom. My favorite moment in this journey was when you said you wanted to be a "comedic author" (not to be confused with author, and okay). I love you. And last but never least, thank you to my copilot, Brenda, for rockin' this out with me!

Brenda would like to thank her friends on Capitol Hill; without your passion and determination to fight legislatively and strategically in this hard time, our democracy might no longer exist. My struggle for you here was to incline this project toward a true representation of your sacrifice, intellect, and capability. To special friends who helped me hang in there: Kathryn Williams, Cheryl Johnson, Shashrina Thomas, Ingrid Gavin-Parks, Kim Ross, Michael Hagbourne, Joan Kelsey, and the DMV Quartet. Thanks to Bernard Demczuk for opening the Growlery at Giverny West whenever I needed quiet concentration. To the absolute best parents—the late Myrtle Bowers Davis and Robert Lee Davis—who instilled in me the highest integrity, the best education, and the richest experiences. To Rep. John Lewis, without whom my career in politics would never have been possible. Thank you for your unwavering faith in me and unyielding commitment to art, inspiration, creativity, justice, and peace.

Thanks to Speaker Nancy Pelosi, Chairwoman Maxine Waters, Sen. Elizabeth Warren, and Rep. Alexandria Ocasio-Cortez for your bright, shining lives of public service. Krishan, Plume, and I can only hope that we have begun to return to you just a small part of what you sacrifice so much to give to us all. Hail the Queens of the Resistance.

To our readers, from our hearts to yours, *thank you, thank you, thank you* for celebrating the Queens of the Resistance series with us!

SOURCES

Arceneaux, Michael. "For the Record, Maxine Waters' Wig Is Better Than Bill O'Reilly's Entire Career." *Essence*, March 29, 2017.

"Aristide Said U.S. Deposed Him in 'Coup D'etat.'" CNN.com. March 1, 2004.

Bandele, Asha. "The Life of an Outlaw." *Vibe*, May 2003.

Bennett, Jessica. "I Am (an Older) Woman. Hear Me Roar." *The New York Times*, January 8, 2019.

Brown, Roxanne. "A Black Woman's Place Is in the . . . House of Representatives." *Ebony*, January 1991.

Brownstein, Ronald. "The Two Worlds of Maxine Waters: Mastering the Back Rooms of Sacramento, Battling Despair on the Streets of L.A." *Los Angeles Times*, March 5, 1989.

Burns, James. "Maxine Waters." *American Government ABC-CLIO*, 2019.

California Legislature. "Assembly Bill No. 607." February 13, 1987.

Camia, Catalina. "Maxine Waters' 'Project Build': Job Training Program Goes Right to the Housing Projects for People." *Los Angeles Times*, December 22, 1985.

Carlos, Marjon. "Congresswoman Maxine Waters Has Always Fought for Women's Rights in Style." *Vogue*, March 29, 2017.

Chicago Tribune. "3 Members in Congress Arrested in Haitian Protest." May 5, 1994.

Collier, Aldore. "Maxine Waters: Telling It Like It Is in L.A." *Ebony*, October 1, 1992.

Congresswoman Maxine Waters. "About Maxine." Accessed February 9, 2020, https://waters.house.gov/about-maxine.

———. "Biography." Accessed February 9, https://waters.house.gov/about-maxine/biography.

———. "Congresswoman Waters Introduces Bill to Protect Poor Countries from Vulture Funds." waters.house.gov, July 30, 2009.

———. "Congresswoman Waters Joins Nancy Pelosi and Elizabeth Warren to Fight for Consumer Protections." waters.house.gov, July 27, 2017.

———. "Congresswoman Waters Reintroduces the Stop AIDS in Prison Act." waters.house.gov, April, 4, 2017.

———. "Congresswoman Waters Supports the Net Neutrality Day of Action and Fights for Internet Freedom and Privacy." waters.house.gov, July 12, 2017.

———. "In Remembrance of Jule Sugarman, Founder of Head Start." waters.house.gov, November 16, 2010.

———. "Out of Iraq Caucus." waters.house.gov, August 6, 2009.

———. "Rep. Maxine Waters Introduces Bill to Remove Mandatory Minimums From Federal Law." waters.house.gov, September 12, 2013.

———. "Rep. Maxine Waters Secures Millions for Projects in CA-35." waters.house.gov, June 15, 2009.

———. "Rep. Waters Statement on the Death of John Conyers Jr." waters.house.gov, October 29, 2019.

———. "Waters Announces Medical Exams for Delta Fuel Dump Families." waters.house.gov, January 24, 2020.

———. "Waters Condemns Donald Trump's Policy of Separating Children from Their Parents at the Border." waters.house.gov, June 20, 2018.

Departments of Labor, Health and Human Services, Education, and Related Agencies Appropriations for 1998. *Hearings*. Government Printing Office, 1987.

Dyson, Michael Eric. *Holler If You Hear Me*. Basic Civitas Books, 2011.

Ebony. "Powercise Regular Workouts Keep Prominent Blacks in the Game." July 1994.

Eisner, Peter. "Exiled Haitian Departs for Jamaica over U.S. Protest." *Washington Post*, March 15, 2004.

Epstein, Jennifer. "Waters: Tea Party Can Go to Hell." *Politico*, August 22, 2011.

Finley, Taryn. "Maxine Waters: '92 LA Rebellion Was a Defining Moment for Black Resistance." *Huffington Post*, April 27, 2017.

Fullwood, Sam, III. "Rep. Waters Labels Bush 'A Racist,' Endorses Clinton." *Los Angeles Times*, July 9, 1992.

Gladstone, Mark. "Maxine Waters Is Already Staking Out Her Claim." *Los Angeles Times*, October 1, 1990.

Go Black Central. "Congresswoman Maxine Waters' Letter to President Fidel Castro on Assata Shakur 1988." GoBlackCentral.com.

Gontcharova, Natalie. "Maxine Waters: Nancy Pelosi Brought Trump to His Knees." Refinery29, January 30, 2019.

Hall, Carla. "Sidney Williams' Unusual Route to Ambassador Post: Appointments: His Nomination Has Drawn Some Critics. But His Biggest Boost May Come from His Wife, Rep. Maxine Waters." *Los Angeles Times*, February 6,1994.

Hayes, Chris. "All in with Chris Hayes." Transcript. MSNBC News, September 25, 2019.

Henderson, Nia-Malika. "Maxine Waters Is Having a Moment." CNN, April 18, 2017.

History, Art & Archives United States House of Representatives. "Waters, Maxine." https://history.house.gov/People/Listing/W /WATERS,-Maxine-(W000187)/

House Financial Services Committee. "Committee Releases 2019 Highlights and Legislative Successes on Behalf of Hardworking Americans." financialservices.house.gov, December 19, 2019.

Huffington Post. "Maxine Waters: John Boehner and Eric Cantor Are 'Demons.'" February 16, 2012.

Jet. "Congresswomen Square Off on Issue of 'Gangsta Rap.'" March 7, 1994.

Jet. "Sidney Williams, Husband of Rep. Maxine Waters, to Be U.S. Envoy to Bahamas." November 8, 1993.

———. "U.S. Rep. Maxine Waters Recalls How Fifth-Grade Teacher Inspired Her." December 12, 1994.

———. "Waters to Lead Black Caucus; Women Make Shift Into Action." December 9, 1996.

Kim, Mallie Jane. "10 Things You Didn't Know About Maxine Waters." *US News & World Report*, August 23, 2010.

Kristof, Nicholas D. "California Senate Passes Bill to Sell Pretoria-Linked Stock." *The New York Times*, August 26, 1986.

Lindsey, Robert. "California's Tough Line on Apartheid." *The New York Times*, August 31, 1986.

Lipton, Eric. "Lawmaker Didn't Break Ethics Rules in Bank Case, Investigator Finds." *The New York Times*, September 21, 2012.

Los Angeles Times. "Child Abuse Prevention Efforts Seen Ineffective." February 24, 1988.

———. "Maxine Waters." May 16, 1995.

Manegold, Catherine S. "Sometimes the Order of the Day Is Just Maintaining Order." *The New York Times*, July 30, 1994.

Marie, Aurielle. "Dear White Men: Don't Dare Come for Maxine Waters' Wig." *Allure*, March 31, 2017.

Meeks, Kenneth. "Back Talk with Maxine Waters." *Black Enterprise*, June 2005.

Meyerson, Collier. "How Maxine Waters Became a Heroine for the Trump Era." *The Nation*, August 23, 2017.

Millner, Denene. "Congresswoman Maxine Waters Speaks Truth to Power: 'Directly, and Aggressively, Without Apology.'" glamour.com. October 30, 2017.

———. "Too Brave to Back Down." *Glamour*, December 2017.

Mills, Kay. "Maxine Waters: 'I Don't Pretend to Be Nice No Matter What . . .'." *The Progressive*, December 1, 1993.

Monk, Janet. "Auntie Maxine Waters Is Reading All Your Tweets." *Lenny Letter*, June 14, 2017.

Muskal, Michael. "Rep. Maxine Waters Says It Is Time for Obama to Fight." *Los Angeles Times*, August 18, 2011.

Newman, Maria. "After the Riots: Washington at Work; Lawmaker from Riot Zone Insists on a New Role for Black Politicians." *The New York Times*, May 19, 1992.

North, Anna. "Maxine Waters' Women's Convention Keynote: 'We're Waging Our Own War Against Rape and Sexual Harassment.'" *Vox*, October 29, 2017.

Ottesen, K K. "Maxine Waters: If I Want to Fight, I Want to Fight with Lions." *The Washington Post*, August 27, 2019.

Penrose, Nerisha. "Congresswoman Maxine Waters Calls Tupac Her Favorite Rapper." *Billboard*, August 7, 2017.

Philips, Chuck. "Rap Finds a Supporter in Rep. Maxine Waters." *Los Angeles Times*, February 15, 1994.

Protess, Ben. "The Mellowing of Maxine Waters." *The New York Times*, May 11, 2013.

Rhimes, Shonda. "Rep. Maxine Waters Spills the Tea." Shondaland .com, September 17, 2017.

Rhodan, Maya. "This Democratic Congresswoman Keeps Bringing Up Impeachment." *Time*, February 2, 2017.

Rias, Hope C. *St. Louis School Desegregation: Patterns of Progress and Peril*. Palgrave Macmillan, 2018.

Ring, Trudy. "An Essential Primer on the Legendary Maxine Waters." *Advocate*, March 31, 2017.

Rye, Angela. "Queen Maxine (Feat. Maxine Waters)." *On One with Angela Rye*. July 11, 2017, https://soundcloud.com/ononewith angelarye/queen-maxine-feat-maxine-waters.

———. "Queen Maxine." *Essence*, December 2017/January 2018.

Sentinel Wire Services. "Waters' Mother Velma Lee Carr Moore Succumbs." *Los Angeles Sentinel*, May 29, 2014.

Sheetz, Michael. "Watch Maxine Waters and Secretary Mnuchin Argue at Hearing: 'I Will Not Be Back Here.'" CNBC, April 10, 2019.

Shuit, Douglas. "Waters Is a Fighter: Ask Any Assemblyman." *Los Angeles Times*, September 11, 1987.

Simon, Richard. "Maxine Waters Accused of Three Ethics Violations." *Los Angeles Times*, August 10, 2010.

Sonenshein, Raphael J. *Politics in Black and White: Race and Power in Los Angeles*. Princeton University Press, 1994.

Stewart, Emily. "'I Have the Gavel': Maxine Waters Lays Out an Aggressive Agenda at the House Financial Services Committee." *Vox*, January 16, 2019.

The History Makers "Ethel Bradley Biography." Accessed March 1, 2020.

———. "The Honorable Maxine Waters: Biography." https://www.thehistorymarkers.org/biography/honorable-maxine-waters.

The YBF. "Rep. Maxine Waters BEEN About That Life—Says Rap Music Shouldn't Be Censored & Tupac Is Her Favorite Rapper." August 7, 2017.

Thomas, Marlo. *The Right Words at the Right Time: Marlo Thomas and Friends*. New York: Atria Books, 2002.

Turner, Deonna S. "Crack Epidemic." Britannica.com.

U.S. News & World Report "These Democratic Lawmakers Won't Attend Trump's Inauguration." January 14, 2017.

"U.S. Rep. Maxine Waters Recalls How Fifth-Grade Teacher Inspired Her." *Jet*. December 12, 1994.

U.S. Senate. "Waters, Maxine." In *Biographical Directory of the United States Congress 1774–Present*. Government Printing Office.

United States Congresswoman Jan Schakowsky. "House Democratic Caucus Special Committee on Election Reform Releases Comprehensive Report on Voting System." https://schakowsky.house.gov/, November 7, 2001.

Warmbrodt, Zachary, and Cristiano Lima. "Maxine Waters Slams Zuckerberg, Raises Specter of Breaking Up Facebook." *Politico*, October 23, 2019.

Warren, Chris. "Running Water." *Los Angeles*. November 1, 1998.

Waters, Maxine. "Maxine Waters on How the Women's March Revived Her Faith in the Younger Generation." *Glamour*, January 20, 2018.

Wiggins, David K. *Out of the Shadows: A Biographical History of African American Athletes*. University of Arkansas Press, 2008.

Wire, Sarah. "How Maxine Waters Became Auntie Maxine in the Age of Trump." *Los Angeles Times*, April 30, 2017.

ABOUT THE AUTHORS

Brenda Jones is best known for her fifteen-year tenure as communications director for an icon of American politics, Rep. John Lewis. All of his published opinions, statements, and speeches, ranging from his introductions of US presidents to commencement addresses delivered to the Ivy League, and those celebrating his transformative Civil Rights legacy were penned by Brenda Jones during that time. She collaborated with him on his book *Across That Bridge: A Vision for Change and the Future of America*, which won an NAACP Image Award. She has also worked in commercial television news and public broadcasting.

Krishan Trotman is an executive editor at Hachette Books, recently profiled in *Essence* magazine as one of the few African American publishing executives. She has committed over fifteen years to publishing books by and about multicultural voices and social justice. Throughout her career as an editor she has proudly worked with leaders and trailblazers on this frontier such as John Lewis, Stephanie Land, Malcolm Nance, Zerlina Maxwell, Ed Gordon, and Lindy West.